asian **apartments**

apartamentos asiáticos

appartamenti in asia

© 2003 Feierabend Verlag OHG
Mommsenstr. 43
D- 10629 Berlin

Traducción del inglés: Silvia Gómez de Antonio & Irene Moreno Palacios
Traduzione dall' inglese: Raffaella Durante-Müller & Eleonora Zoratti
Typesetting of the trilingual edition: adHOC Laureck & Beuster oHG

Editorial director: Kelley Cheng
Photography: Kelley Cheng (unless otherwise stated)
Art director: Jacinta Neoh
Sub-editors/writers: Hwee-Chuin Ang & Narelle Yakuba
Graphic designers: Chai-Yen Wong & Sharn Selina Lim

Co-ordinators:
Anna Koor (Hong Kong, China)
Savinee Buranasilapin (Bangkok, Thailand)
Thomas Dannecker (Bangkok, Thailand)

Colour separation: SC Graphic Technology Pte Ltd

Asian Apartments
First published in Singapore in 2003
by Page One Publishing Private Limited
Text & Photography © copyright 2003 Page One Publishing Private Limited

Printing and Binding: Stampa Nazionale s.r.l., Italy

Printed in Italy
ISBN 3-936761-27-2
37 07016 1

On the cover
Designed by Joey Ho (HK)
Photography by Kelley Cheng

asian **apartments**
apartamentos asiáticos
appartamenti in asia

Feierabend

contents
sumario
sommario

introduction
introducción
introduzione

If you were to think of Asian living, it is likely that two images would spring to mind – one is the palette of centuries old Asian building techniques for housing; with, for example, a rich and multi-layered courtyard house in China containing a processional unfolding of spaces punctuated by gateways; a sparse, subtle and flexible house in Japan with an almost religious aesthetic; clusters of courtyard houses in India; or a Malay house, raised on stilts with an open plan, and designed to perfectly suit the tropical climate. You would probably think of local materials such as timber, bamboo and rattan, and the techniques that have evolved for both constructing and decorating with them. You might also think of Asian religions, cultural traditions and rituals, and their poetic effect on the design and use of the house.

On the other hand, if you think of Asian living, you might see an image of dense urbanity; a landscape of high-rise apartment blocks containing large populations living close together in small spaces, with fast-paced lifestyles and an adoption of Western habits and products. In this case you might think of cities such as Hong Kong, Tokyo or Singapore, whose voracious economies are based on industry rather than traditional modes of production and trade. Arguably, this second model for living is the one that will take precedence into the future, as populations continue to migrate from the countryside to the city in search of work in industry.

The Asian apartments presented in this book are exemplary of current trends in the design of apartments in Asia. Some of the apartments are imbued with a sense of the Asian building tradition – in both a tangible and intangible manner – expressing a real appreciation of the subtle experiential and perceptual occupation of space as well as physical aspects of Asian building traditions. These examples manage to draw inspiration from the past whilst embracing the future. Some of the apartments included in this book have achieved an Asian flavour with the careful inclusion of Asian furnishings and decorative elements. Others still are reflective of a universal design sensibility – rational, simple and functional – and are thereby representative of the new direction of informal modern living in Asian cities.

Si usted tuviera que pensar en la vida asiática, seguramente le vendrían dos ideas a la cabeza; una, la gama de técnicas asiáticas centenarias para la construcción de casas, como por ejemplo en China, con casas estratificadas y jardines interiores y en las que los espacios se despliegan en cadena interrumpidos por puertas abiertas, o en el Japón, con sus casas austeras, delicadas y flexibles y su estética fundamentalmente religiosa; los grupos de casas con jardines interiores en la India o las casas malayas, construidas sobre pilotes, de plano abierto y diseñadas para adaptarse perfectamente al clima tropical. Probablemente piense en materiales como la madera, el bambú y la rota, y en las técnicas desarrolladas para construir y decorar con estas materias. Puede que también piense en las religiones asiáticas, en las tradiciones culturales y rituales, y en su poético efecto sobre el diseño y el uso de la casa.

Por otro lado, si usted piensa en la vida asiática, posiblemente vea una imagen de densa urbanización; un paisaje de altos bloques de apartamentos albergando a una gran cantidad de personas que viven apiñadas en pequeños espacios, con un acelerado ritmo de vida y una adopción de costumbres y productos occidentales. En este sentido seguramente esté usted pensando en ciudades como Hong Kong, Tokio o Singapur, cuyas voraces economías están basadas en la industria más que en modos de producción y comercio tradicionales. Posiblemente sea este segundo modelo de vida el que prevalezca en el futuro si la población continúa emigrando del campo a la ciudad en busca de trabajo en la industria.

Los apartamentos asiáticos recogidos en esta obra presentan de forma ejemplar las tendencias actuales en el diseño de apartamentos en Asia. Algunos de ellos están empapados de la sensibilidad de la tradición constructora asiática – de una forma tangible e intangible – expresando una comprensión real de la sutil ocupación experimental y perceptiva del espacio además de los aspectos físicos de las tradiciones constructoras asiáticas. Estos ejemplos logran encontrar la inspiración en el pasado y abrazan, al mismo tiempo, el futuro. Algunos de los apartamentos incluidos en este libro han conseguido un toque asiático gracias a la cuidadosa inclusión de muebles y elementos decorativos asiáticos. Otros siguen reflejando la sensibilidad de diseño universal (racional, simple y funcional) y son por eso representativos de la nueva forma de vida informal en las ciudades asiáticas.

Quando si pensa allo stile di vita in Asia sono quasi sempre due le immagini che subito vengono in mente: da una parte la grande varietà delle antiche forme costruttive asiatiche, come la casa con cortile cinese, sontuosa e a più piani, al cui interno si susseguono come in processione spazi aperti, interrotti qua e là da portoni; oppure una casa giapponese, sottile, delicata, flessibile, dall'estetica quasi religiosa; o anche gruppi di case con cortile in India; o ancora una casa malese, una palafitta dalla pianta aperta, creata per armonizzarsi perfettamente al clima tropicale. Si pensa poi probabilmente a materiali tipici, legno, bambù e rattan e alle tecniche per sfruttarli sia nel campo costruttivo che in quello decorativo. Vengono in mente le religioni asiatiche, le tradizioni culturali e i rituali e il loro effetto poetico nella progettazione e nell'utilizzo delle abitazioni.

Dall'altra parte, quando si pensa allo stile di vita in Asia si pensa anche a città densamente popolate, a palazzoni di più appartamenti, stracolmi di persone che vivono l'una appiccicata all'altra, con uno stile di vita esagitato e abitudini e mode occidentali. In questo caso si penserà a città come Hong Kong, Tokyo o Singapore, città dal sistema economico vorace, basato più sull'industria che su modalità di produzione e commercio tradizionali. Non c'è dubbio, del resto, che questo secondo modello sia quello che, vista la continua e massiccia emigrazione dalle campagne verso le città industriali, si imporrà in futuro.

Quelle presentate in questo libro sono testimonianze delle tendenze attuali nella progettazione di appartamenti in Asia. Alcune abitazioni rievocano le tecniche tradizionali di costruzione, sia dal punto di vista più direttamente materiale che da quello spirituale, rivalutando l'ingegnosa divisione dello spazio e la direzione nell'esposizione, della tipica tecnica costruttiva asiatica. Sono esempi di appartamenti che riescono a trarre ispirazione dal passato e nel contempo abbracciano il futuro. Alcuni degli appartamenti presentati in questo libro hanno acquisito un'atmosfera asiatica grazie all'arredamento e agli elementi decorativi. Altri rispecchiano invece una sensibilità di ideazione universale, razionale, semplice e funzionale, e sono perciò rappresentativi del nuovo indirizzo delle città asiatiche verso uno stile moderno e informale.

PROGRESSION

vestibules and corridors

Much of traditional Asian domestic architecture is based on the concept of processional space – a subtle unfolding of the private realm as one progresses through the space of the house from the exterior world. As transitional, in-between realms, corridors typically address the sensory as well as perform the physical function of transporting the body from one space to another.

PROGRESIÓN

vestíbulos y pasillos

Gran parte de la arquitectura doméstica tradicional asiática está basada en el concepto del despliegue de los espacios, una sutil abertura del ámbito privado a medida que uno se adentra en el espacio de la casa desde el mundo exterior. Como zonas de transición —entre dos reinos—, los pasillos suelen atender no sólo a lo sensorial, sino que además realizan la función física de transportar el cuerpo de un espacio a otro.

SUCCESSIONE

anticamera e corridoio

Gran parte dell'architettura domestica asiatica è basata su un concetto di concatenazione degli spazi, un delicato rivelarsi del regno privato, come una sorta di lento avanzamento del mondo esterno attraverso lo spazio della casa. Come reami di transizione, nel mezzo, i corridoi sono guide dei sensi; adempiono inoltre alla funzione pratica di spazi attraverso cui ci si sposta da una camera all'altra.

Entry halls and corridors carry out an interesting double life. Whilst they welcome and carry you through space, transporting you from public zones to the innermost private areas of the home, they are really a non-place, being devoid of permanent occupation. Vestibules and corridors are spaces for movement. As such, they offer the opportunity for interesting architectural explorations to do with progression and theatrics. The vestibules and corridors illustrated in this chapter show a variety of ways of dealing with the transitional zones of vestibules and corridors in apartments. Some very interesting solutions involve the employment of meandering passages and indirect lines of sight to create an unfolding process as one proceeds through the space. Such weaving and layering can prompt a real sense of anticipation of what lies ahead, as well as add life and intrigue to a space of this singular function.

Los vestíbulos de la entrada y los pasillos tienen una interesante doble vida. Además de darle la bienvenida y de conducirle a través del espacio, transportándole de las zonas públicas a los lugares privados de la casa, son, al mismo tiempo, lugares inexistentes desprovistos de una ocupación permanente. Los vestíbulos y los pasillos son espacios para el movimiento. Así, ofrecen la posibilidad de realizar interesantes estudios arquitectónicos con la progresión y la teatralidad.
Los vestíbulos y los pasillos que se ilustran en este capítulo muestran varias posibilidades de empleo de estas zonas de transición en los apartamentos. Algunas soluciones, muy interesantes, implican el uso de pasillos sinuosos y de líneas indirectas para crear una sensación de despliegue a medida que se avanza a través del espacio. Esta forma serpenteante y angulosa de recorrer el espacio puede provocar un verdadero sentimiento de anticipación respecto a lo que se va a encontrar más adelante, además de proporcionarle vida e intriga a este espacio de función tan particular.

Anticamere e corridoi hanno una doppia funzione oltremodo interessante. Sebbene accolgano l'ospite e lo guidino attraverso lo spazio, conducendolo dalle zone «pubbliche» agli angoli più intimi della casa, in realtà non sono vere e proprie stanze, ma solo zone di passaggio. Anticamere e corridoi rappresentano il movimento e offrono grazie a questa loro particolarità la possibilità di interessanti esperimenti architettonici sul tema della successione e della rappresentazione teatrale dello spazio. Le anticamere e i corridoi presentati in questo capitolo sono una scelta di soluzioni mirate a collegare tra loro le varie camere di un appartamento. Alcune, molto interessanti, implicano l'uso di passaggi serpeggianti e scorci visivi indiretti per trasmettere la sensazione del lento schiudersi dello spazio, come una sorta di conquista graduale. Questo procedere serpeggiante e a tappe può suggerire un'anticipazione di ciò che c'e alla fine del cammino, oltre a regalare un po' di vita e intrigo a uno spazio che di per sé ha un'unica funzione.

Meandering passages and indirect lines.
of sight create an unfolding process.
as one proceeds through the space.

Pasajes sinuosos y líneas de visión indirectas
crean un proceso de despliegue a medida que se
avanza a través del espacio.

Passaggi serpeggianti e scorci visivi indiretti
trasmettono la sensazione del lento schiudersi
dello spazio, come una sorta di conquista
attraverso di esso.

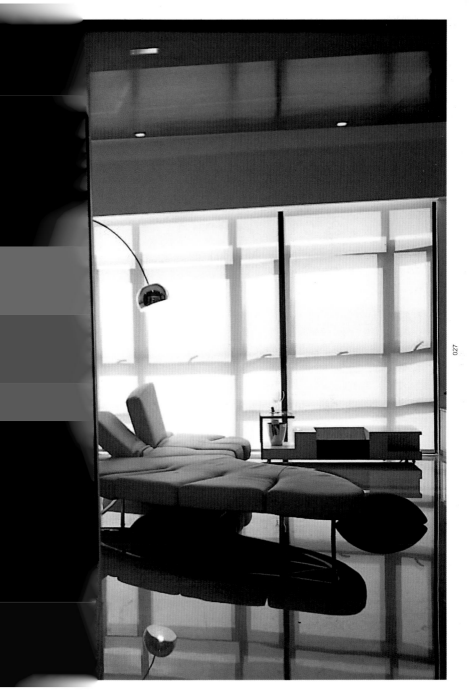

Corridors can become dramatic interludes between rooms.

Los pasillos pueden convertirse en interludios dramáticos entre las habitaciones.

I corridoi si trasformano in un intermezzo drammatico tra le stanze.

INTERAKTION
living rooms

Living rooms in traditional Asian dwellings vary in size and formality according to different cultures. In Chinese houses, for example, the living room has traditionally been a formal room to receive and entertain guests, with a somewhat ceremonial selection and layout of furniture. A Malay house, usually with an open plan and fewer pieces of furniture, may somewhat connote a more informal and flexible gathering space.

INTERACCIÓN
salones

Los salones en las viviendas asiáticas tradicionales varían de tamaño y de forma según las diferentes culturas. En las casas chinas, por ejemplo, el salón era tradicionalmente una habitación formal para recibir y atender a las visitas, con unos muebles seleccionados y dispuestos de una forma un tanto ceremonial. Una casa malaya con una distribución abierta y menos mobiliario puede connotar un espacio de reunión más informal y flexible.

INTERAZIONE
soggiorno

I soggiorni delle abitazioni tradizionali asiatiche variano in grandezza e struttura in base alle diverse culture. Nelle case cinesi, per esempio, il soggiorno è una vera e propria stanza di ricevimento per accogliere e intrattenere gli ospiti, caratterizzato da una scelta e una disposizione dell'arredamento alquanto formale. La casa malese, invece, con la sua pianta a schema aperto e lo scarso mobilio, incarna la ricerca di uno spazio di incontro più informale e flessibile.

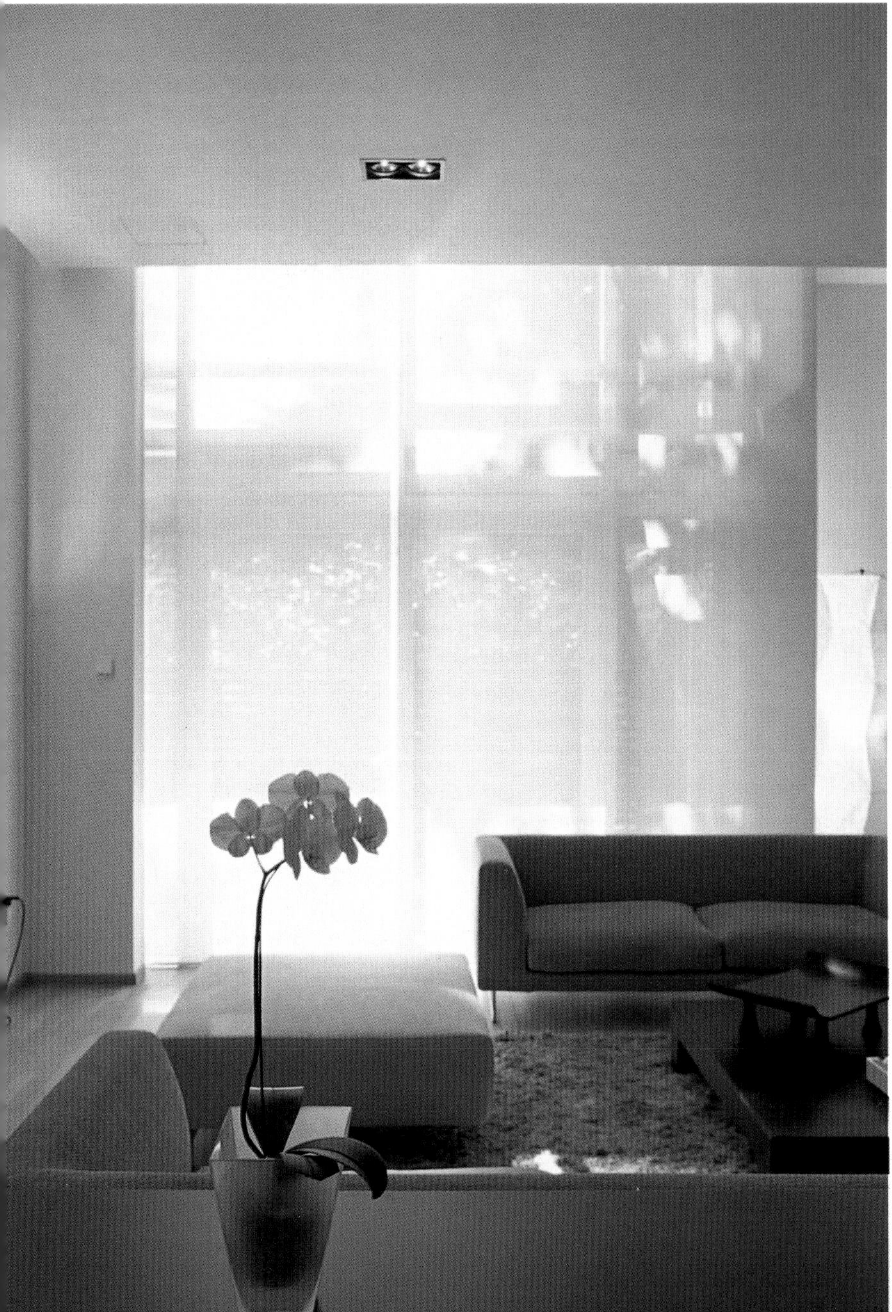

The living room itself has really become the heart of the modern home. Particularly in apartments, the living room is typically the main space where not only the home occupants relax and interact, but is also where they receive and entertain guests. It is a place that must be comfortable and expressive of the occupants' tastes, and have a level of formality that suits their lifestyle and entertaining needs. Whilst houses traditionally contain a formal sitting room with the dedicated function of receiving guests, the smaller apartments do not allow for this. Changing lifestyles are also outmoding the concept of a formal sitting room; as we become busier and our routines become more varied, there are lesser opportunities for formal gatherings. The living room must thus be supportive of the dual function of being both a relaxing haven away from the world, and a space that is supportive of social interaction.

El salón mismo se ha convertido en el verdadero corazón de la casa moderna. Especialmente en los apartamentos, el salón es por norma general el espacio principal en el que no sólo se relajan y se relacionan los habitantes de una casa, sino que además es el lugar en el que se recibe y atiende a los invitados. Es un espacio que debe ser confortable y expresar el gusto de los residentes, y posee un nivel de formalidad ajustado al estilo de vida y a las necesidades de atender a sus invitados. Mientas que las casas tradicionales disponen de un salón formal dedicado a la función de recibir a los visitantes, el espacio, más reducido, de los apartamentos no lo permite. Un estilo de vida cada vez más diferente está desplazando el concepto del salón formal como algo pasado de moda; como cada vez estamos más ocupados y nuestra rutina es cada vez más variada, hay menos ocasiones para las reuniones formales. El salón debe servir, por lo tanto, de apoyo a esta doble función: ser un lugar en el que poder relajarse alejándose del mundo exterior y, además, ser un espacio apropiado para las relaciones sociales.

Il soggiorno è divenuto il cuore della casa moderna. Soprattutto negli appartamenti esso è la zona più importante, dove ci si rilassa, si chiacchiera e dove vengono ricevuti e intrattenuti gli ospiti. Deve essere uno spazio comodo che rispecchia il gusto dei padroni di casa, con un grado di eleganza tale da accordarsi al loro stile di vita e alle esigenze dell'ospitalità. Mentre le case sono tradizionalmente fornite di un tale soggiorno convenzionale atto anche a ricevere gli ospiti, gli appartamenti, più piccoli, non sempre lo permettono. Lo stile di vita però è ormai cambiato e il concetto stesso di soggiorno formale è diventato fuori moda. I nuovi ritmi di vita frenetici hanno diminuito le occasioni di ricevimenti formali; il soggiorno quindi deve oggi soddisfare le due esigenze primarie della vita moderna: deve essere una stanza in cui rilassarsi lontano dalla frenesia del mondo esterno ma dove sia possibile anche ricevere gli amici.

The living room must have a somewhat focal and intimate dimension to it.

El salón debe poseer una cierta dimensión central e íntima.

Il soggiorno ha un'importanza centrale e deve essere soprattutto accogliente.

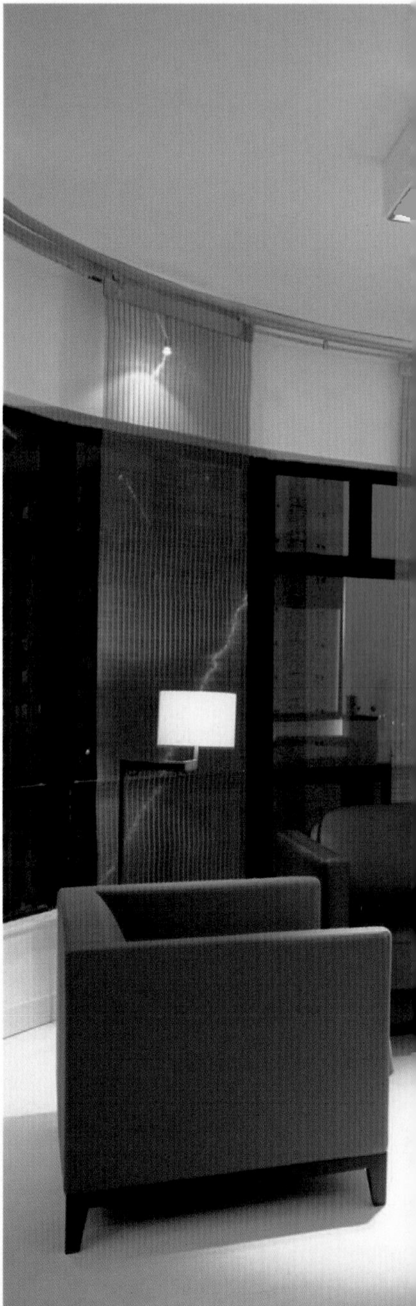

As our lifestyles become busier and our routines more varied, the concept of a formal sitting room being outmoded.

Un estilo de vida más atareado y una rutina cada vez más variada hacen que el concepto del salón formal se convierta en algo anticuado.

Lo stile di vita è cambiato e il concetto stesso di soggiorno formale è diventato fuori moda.

The approach of the open plan for
communal spaces in residential design
is widely adopted today.

El planteamiento del plano abierto para los
espacios comunes en el diseño residencial es
el que generalmente se adopta hoy en día.

Oggi viene ampiamente adottato uno schema
aperto nella progettazione di spazi abitativi comuni.

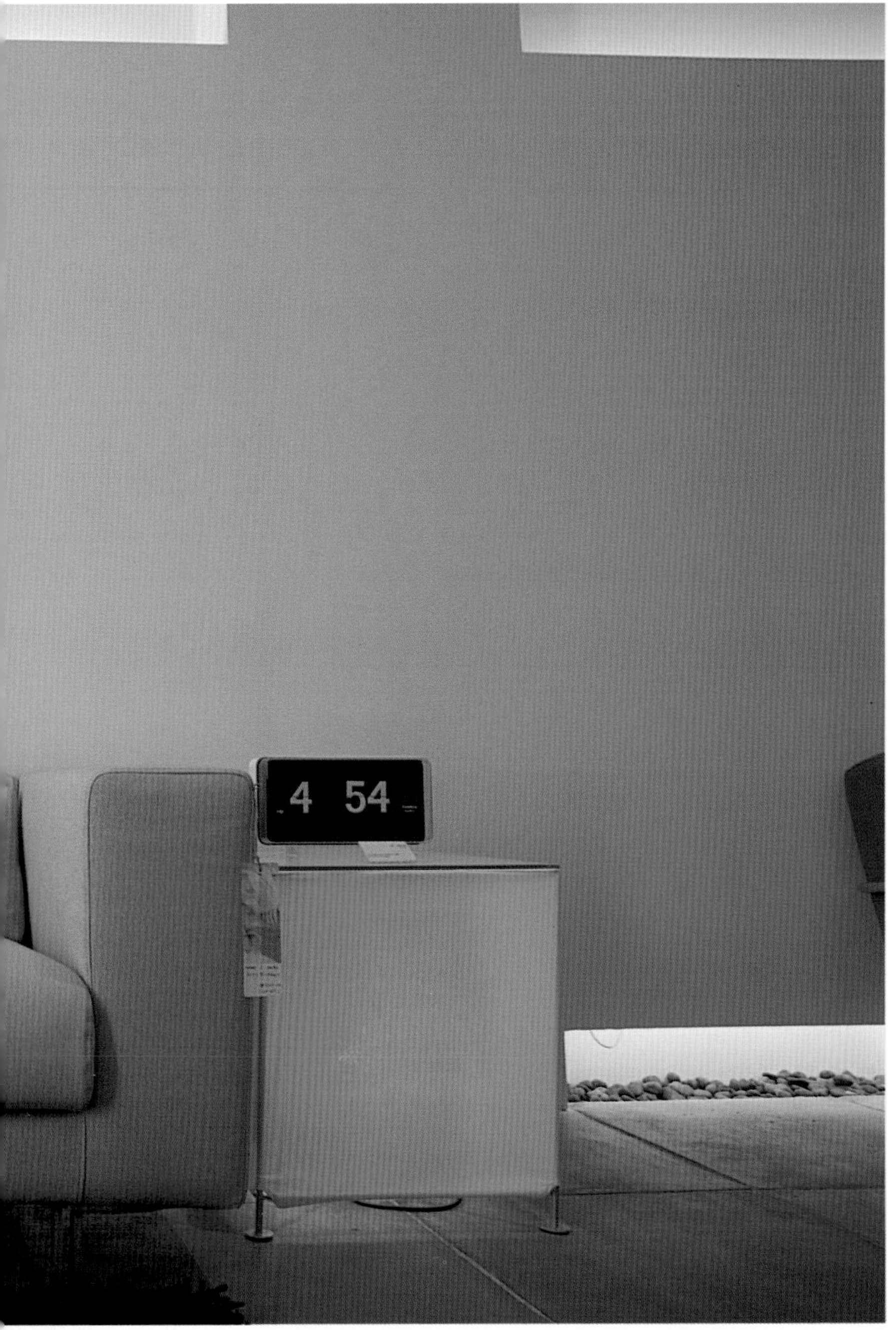
4 54

The living room is a place that must be comfortable and expressive of the occupants' tastes, and have a level of formality that suits their lifestyle and entertaining needs.

El salón es un lugar que debe ser confortable además de expresión del gusto de los residentes, y posee un nivel de formalidad ajustado a su estilo de vida y a las necesidades de atender a sus invitados.

Il soggiorno deve essere uno spazio comodo che rispecchia il gusto dei padroni di casa, con un grado di eleganza tale da accordarsi al loro stile di vita e alle esigenze dell'ospitalità.

CONVERSATION

dining rooms

In all cultures, food brings people together. In Asian cultures, eating is traditionally a social and somewhat ritualistic experience, with the sharing of dishes and beverages, and a rather gradual process of consumption mixed with conversation. The evening has traditionally been an important time of the day, when the whole family is united over a meal.

CONVERSACIÓN

comedores

En todas las culturas la comida es la que reúne a las personas. En las culturas asiáticas, comer es tradicionalmente una experiencia social y en cierta medida ritual, con el reparto de la comida, la bebida y el proceso más bien gradual de la consumición de la comida y que se mezcla con la conversación. La tarde ha sido tradicionalmente un momento importante del día en el que toda la familia se encuentra unida alrededor de la comida.

CONVERSAZIONE

sala da pranzo

In tutte le culture del mondo si mangia volentieri in compagnia. Nelle culture del mondo asiatico i pasti sono eventi sociali con un aspetto estremamente ritualistico, in cui si condividono cibi e bevande, oltre che un momento in cui si consumano i pasti conversando in tranquillità. La sera rispecchia tradizionalmente il momento più importante in cui l'intera famiglia si riunisce per mangiare insieme.

Less predictable modern lifestyles often dictate irregular eating habits – dining out, or dining at home at irregular times. The television has also threatened the demise of the family dinner ritual and breakfast bars have become a convenient place to eat in the morning. Whilst the dining room was once a separate room, where the family would meet at a fixed time and dine together, it is now often an open space sandwiched between the kitchen and living room. Yet, the dining table remains an integral part of the home. It joins the living room in its importance as a focal point.

Depending on the size of your apartment, you may or may not have the space to afford a separate room for dining. The decision on whether or not to enclose the dining room has also a lot to do with the level of formality that you place on the dining ritual. If dining together with your family, or holding formal dinner parties is of importance to you, enclosure of the dining room is a good way to shut out distractions, so that food and conversation can be the focus.

El estilo de vida moderno, menos predecible que antes, impone a menudo hábitos de comida irregulares, como el comer fuera o comer en casa pero a diferentes horas según los días. La televisión también ha puesto en peligro la comida como ritual familiar, y las cafeterías se han convertido en el lugar apropiado para desayunar por las mañanas. Mientras que antiguamente el comedor era una habitación separada en la que la familia se reunía a unas horas fijas para comer junta, hoy en día es, a menudo, un espacio entre la cocina y el salón. Ahora la mesa del comedor parece una parte integrante de la casa. Sin embargo, la mesa del comedor sigue siendo una parte integral de la casa y, junto con el salón, constituye el foco principal.

En función del tamaño de su apartamento, puede que usted disponga o no de un espacio separado para las comidas. La decisión de cerrar o no el comedor depende en gran medida del nivel de formalidad que para usted revista el ritual de la comida. Si considera que comer con su familia o que celebrar comidas formales es algo importante, entonces el incluir un comedor separado es una buena forma de evitar distracciones durante estas reuniones, de modo que la comida y la conversación sean el foco principal.

Lo stile di vita moderno, che non lascia spazio a una rigida programmazione della giornata, spesso impone abitudini alimentari irregolari; si mangia fuori o si mangia a casa ma a orari sempre diversi. La televisione minaccia la fine della rituale cena in famiglia e la colazione viene ormai consumata comodamente seduti al bar.

Mentre una volta la sala da pranzo era una stanza a sé della casa dove la famiglia si incontrava a orari fissi per mangiare insieme, ora è spesso uno spazio aperto schiacciato tra la cucina e il soggiorno. Eppure, il tavolo da pranzo rimane ancora oggi parte essenziale dell'arredamento e mette in risalto l'importanza della sala da pranzo quale punto focale della casa.

In base alla grandezza dell'appartamento, si può avere – ma è raro – spazio sufficiente per adibire un'intera stanza a sala da pranzo. La decisione se allestire o no una sala da pranzo dipende anche molto dall'importanza che si dà al rituale del mangiare insieme. Qualora si dia importanza ai pasti comuni, se si invitano volentieri amici a mangiare, allora una sala da pranzo separata dalle altre stanze è un'ottima idea per concentrare l'attenzione sul cibo e sulla conversazione senza distrazioni.

Less predictable modern lifestyles often dictate irregular eating habits. Yet the dining table remains an integral part of the home.

El estilo de vida moderno, menos predecible que antes, impone a menudo hábitos de comida irregulares. Sin embargo, la mesa del comedor sigue siendo una parte integrante de la casa.

Lo stile di vita moderno, che non lascia spazio a una rigida programmazione della giornata, spesso impone abitudini alimentari irregolari. Eppure il tavolo da pranzo rimane ancora oggi parte essenziale dell'arredamento.

To bring a sense of focus to dining rooms that are not enclosed, lighting can be employed to great effect.

Para lograr centrar la atención en un comedor que no esté en un espacio cerrado, se puede utilizar la iluminación y conseguir así grandes efectos.

Per sottolineare l'importanza di sale da pranzo aperte, l'illuminazione può essere di grande aiuto, regalando fantastici effetti.

The decision on whether or not to enclose
the dining room also has a lot to do with the level
of formality that you place on the dining ritual.

La decisión de cerrar o no el comedor depende
en gran medida del nivel de formalidad que para
usted tenga el ritual de la comida.

La decisione se allestire o no una stanza a sala da
pranzo dipende anche molto dall'importanza che
si dà al rituale del mangiare insieme.

CREATION

kitchens

With its wide plethora of cooking methods and ingredients, Asian cooking is a busy, colourful, fragrant and often energetic affair. The kitchen in many Asian homes has traditionally been located in a peripheral position, in a courtyard, or even in a separate building.

CREACIÓN

cocinas

Con sus abundantes formas de cocinar e ingredientes, la cocina asiática es una aventura laboriosa, llena de colorido, aromática y, a menudo, energética. Tradicionalmente, la cocina se encontraba en muchas casas asiáticas en una posición periférica, en un patio o incluso en un edificio adyacente.

CREAZIONE

cucina

Con la grande varietà di metodi e di ingredienti, cucinare in Asia si rivela un'occupazione impegnativa, colorata, profumata nonché stimolante. Le cucine in molte case asiatiche sono tradizionalmente sistemate in una posizione periferica, in cortile o addirittura in un altro edificio.

Open-plan apartments and houses have done wonders for the kitchen, removing it from a place of lonely isolation, and uniting it with other communal spaces in the home. The kitchen is no longer a purely functional space, but has become a place where people can interact and be creative together.

As domestic roles and lifestyles have changed over the last thirty to forty years, the kitchen has been transformed from a cave of modular formation to a showcase of clean, open lines. Whilst the design of the kitchen must obviously respect functional requirements, it is becoming increasingly common to find that the kitchen is an extension of the living room. The chef in the family is no longer tucked away, but is able to socialise with other members of the family or guests while preparing meals.

En los apartamentos de plano abierto y en las casas se han hecho maravillas para la cocina, se la ha sacado de su lugar de solitario aislamiento y se la ha unido al resto de los lugares comunes de la casa. La cocina ha dejado de ser un espacio puramente funcional para convertirse en un sitio en el que las personas pueden reunirse para comunicarse y ser creativas juntas.

El cambio de los papeles domésticos y del estilo de vida que ha tenido lugar durante los últimos treinta o cuarenta años, ha hecho que la cocina pasase de ser una cueva de estructura modular a un escaparate de líneas abiertas y limpias. Aunque el diseño de la cocina debe respetar los requisitos funcionales, cada vez se generaliza más la concepción de la cocina como una extensión del salón. Al cocinero ya no lo encontramos escondido en la cocina sino que se relaciona con los otros miembros de la familia o con los invitados mientras prepara las comida.

Gli appartamenti e le case a pianta aperta hanno comportato un cambiamento fondamentale nel posizionamento della cucina, privandola del suo splendido isolamento e unendola ad altri spazi comuni nella casa. La cucina non è più uno spazio puramente funzionale, ma è diventata un luogo in cui ci si può incontrare, conversare e creare insieme.

Quando negli ultimi trenta o quaranta anni i ruoli domestici e lo stile di vita sono cambiati, la cucina si è trasformata da caverna di elementi componibili in vetrina di strutture pulite e aperte. Pur essendo chiaro che la progettazione delle cucine deve rispettare esigenze strettamente funzionali, si va affermando la tendenza a considerare queste stanze come prolungamenti del soggiorno. Il cuoco della famiglia non se ne deve stare più nascosto, ma può preparare i pasti stando tranquillamente in compagnia di familiari e ospiti.

Cooking itself, has recently gained popularity as a «lifestyle» activity, and an attractive and accessible kitchen is rapidly becoming a requirement in the home.

El cocinar en sí ha ganado popularidad como una actividad propia del «estilo de vida»; una cocina interesante y accesible se está convirtiendo rápidamente en algo indispensable en la casa.

Cucinare è ormai diventata un'attività di moda e una cucina bella e funzionale si è velocemente trasformata in un requisito irrinunciabile della casa.

It is becoming increasingly common to find that the kitchen is an extension of the living room.

Cada vez se generaliza más la concepción de la cocina como una extensión del salón.

Sta diventando sempre più di moda considerare le cucine come prolungamenti del soggiorno.

RELAXATION

bedrooms

Peace is extolled in Asian cultures. The bedroom, having replaced the traditional courtyard as the deepest and innermost sanctuary of the domestic sphere, provides a site for recuperation, relaxation and contemplation.

RELAJACIÓN

dormitorios

Las culturas asiáticas ensalzan la paz. El dormitorio, habiendo reemplazado al patio tradicional como santuario más íntimo y secreto de la esfera doméstica, ofrece un lugar para la recuperación, la relajación y la contemplación.

RELAX

camera da letto

Le culture asiatiche amano e rispettano la pace. La camera da letto, offrendo un luogo di riposo, relax e contemplazione, si è ormai impossessata del primato che una volta aveva il cortile quale il più sacro e intimo santuario della sfera domestica.

When it comes to the bedroom, comfort and tactility assume importance as the motivating forces on design. The essential function of the private realm of the bedroom is to restore both the body and mind. So the design style of the bedroom should derive naturally from a consideration of building materials, fabrics, lighting and colours – all the elements that will contribute to the creation of a comfortable private retreat.

Levels of enclosure can also be explored in the treatment of windows. Soft, translucent curtains will offer a degree of privacy, whilst allowing natural light to enter the room. If wanted, block out curtains will completely shut out the world. Many apartment towers offer the opportunity for breathtaking views, in which you may find respose.

En el dormitorio, el confort y el sentido del tacto son más relevantes que la motivación del diseño. La función esencial de este reino privado del dormitorio es la de procurar el descanso del cuerpo y de la mente. Por eso, el estilo del diseño del dormitorio debería resultar, naturalmente, de la consideración de los materiales, la fabricación de los elementos, la iluminación y el color; es decir, de todos los elementos que contribuirán a la creación de un confortable refugio privado.

El acondicionamiento de las ventanas permite explorar los diferentes ambientes de la habitación. Unas cortinas ligeras y translúcidas dan cierta privacidad y, además, permiten el paso de la luz natural. Al cerrarlas, podemos dejar fuera el mundo. Muchas torres de apartamentos ofrecen la posibilidad de disfrutar de bellas vistas y son ideales para el descanso.

Quando si tratta di progettare una camera da letto sono la comodità e il piacere al tatto i criteri più importanti da seguire. La funzione principale di questo reame privato è quella di ristorare il corpo e la mente. Per questo è importante che nel progettare le camere da letto si valutino bene i materiali di costruzione, i tessuti, le luci e i colori, tutti elementi che contribuiscono alla creazione di un luogo veramente confortevole in cui ritirarsi.

La scelta del tipo di tende alle finestre varia in base al grado di isolamento dal mondo esterno che si vuole ottenere. Tende leggere e translucide garantiranno una certa privacy, pur permettendo alla luce naturale di entrare nella stanza. Se invece lo si desidera, si potrà escludere del tutto il mondo esterno grazie a tende più spesse. Molti appartamenti in grandi residence offrono angoli con un panorama rilassante, ideali per sistemarci una camera da letto.

Many apartment towers offer the opportunity for breathtaking views, in which you may find repose.

Muchas torres de apartamentos ofrecen la posibilidad de disfrutar de bellas vistas y son ideales para el descanso.

Molti appartamenti in grandi residence offrono angoli con un panorama rilassante, ideali per sistemarci una camera da letto.

Sensuous effects can be achieved
by mixing fabric textures on the bed.

Se pueden conseguir efectos sensuales
mezclando materiales de diferentes
texturas en la cama.

Sul letto si ottengono
effetti piacevoli abbinando
tessuti a trama diversa.

The essential function of the private realm of the bedroom is to restore both the body and mind.

La función esencial de este reino privado es la de procurar el descanso del cuerpo y de la mente.

La funzione principale di questo reame privato è quella di ristorare il corpo e la mente.

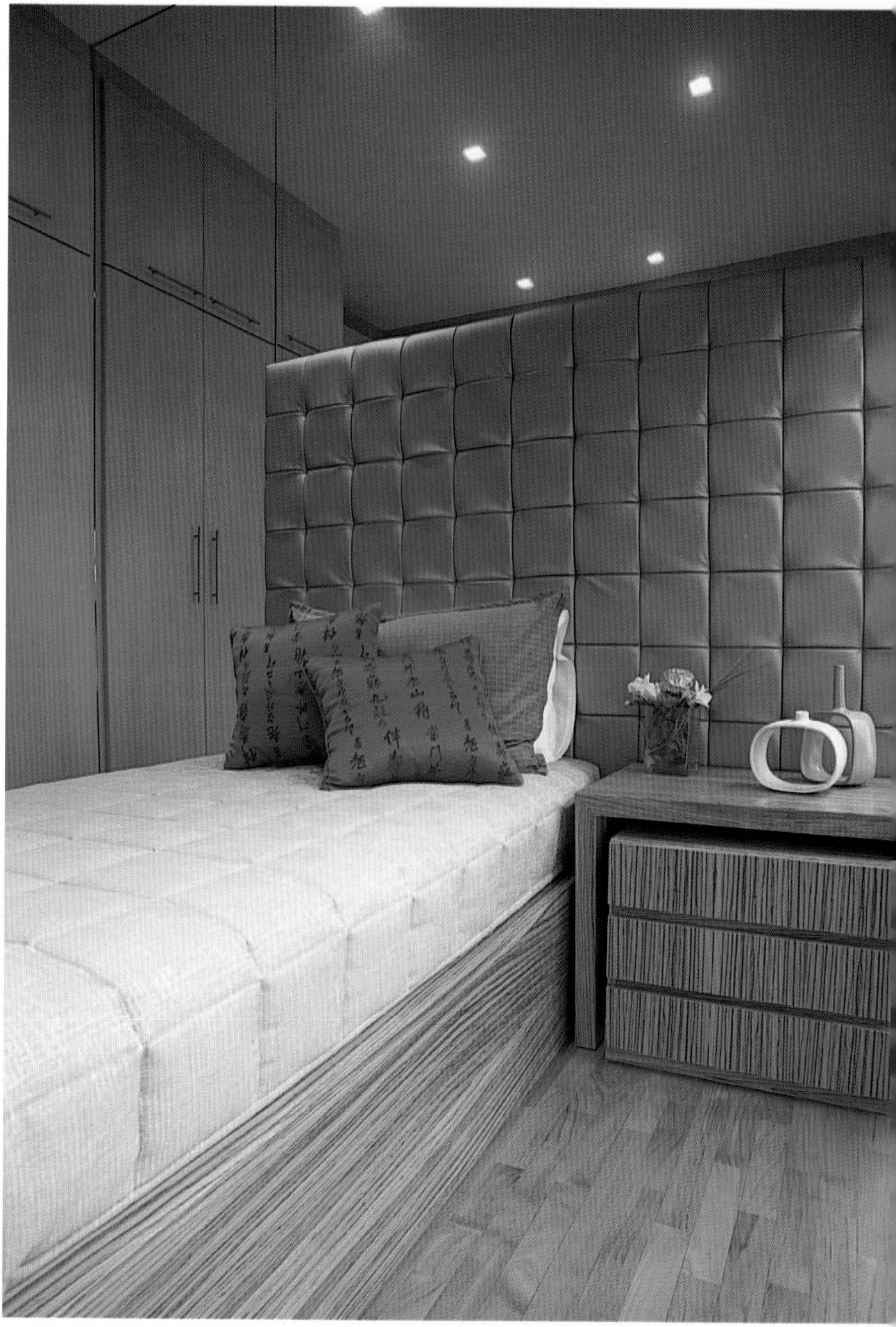

If lighting is kept dim, there will be more focus on the physical senses – on bodily comfort and tactile sensation.

Una luz tenue centra más la atención en los sentidos físicos; en el bienestar del cuerpo y en la sensibilidad del tacto.

La luce soffusa acuisce i sensi; si gode della comodità e della morbidezza dei tessuti.

CONTEMPLATION

bathrooms

Rituals are an integral part of the traditional Asian way of life. But rituals in contemporary Asian living have taken on new meanings. Modern day rituals have less to do with mysticism and spirituality, but are based instead on day-to-day habitual activities like tea drinking and bathing.

CONTEMPLACIÓN

cuartos de baño

Los rituales son una parte esencial de la forma de vida asiática tradicional. Sin embargo, estos rituales han tomado un nuevo significado en la vida asiática contemporánea. Hoy en día estos ceremoniales no tienen tanto que ver con el misticismo o con la espiritualidad, sino que están basados en actividades diarias como beber té o bañarse.

RACCOGLIMENTO

bagno

I rituali sono parte integrante dello stile di vita asiatico, anche se nella vita asiatica contemporanea hanno acquisito nuovi significati. Questi moderni rituali non hanno più nulla di mistico o spirituale; dettano invece il ritmo di attività quotidiane abituali, come bere il tè o fare il bagno.

A lack of space is one of the major concerns when designing a bathroom in an apartment. If you are short of space, the use of frosted glass or glass bricks to enclose the bathroom from the next room will still ensure privacy, but the transmission of light will assist in making the bathroom feel larger. Applying a large mirror, or even covering the whole wall above the basin with mirror, will also have the visual effect of room enlargement. Flooding the room with natural light through extensive fenestration will increase the feeling of spaciousness as well.

Artificial lighting in the bathroom can be used copiously to create a full and warm environment, or can be dimmed with just the essential areas such as the basin or feature shelves highlighted. Today's wide selection of tiles offers the potential for interesting textural effects. You can choose to tile walls right up to the ceiling, or just to dado height. Be sure to allow yourself sufficient storage capacity, so that visual clutter from bathroom products can be minimised.

La falta de espacio en los apartamentos es uno de los mayores problemas a la hora de diseñar el baño. Si este es su caso, la construcción de paredes de cristal esmerilado o de ladrillos de cristal para separar el baño de la habitación contigua, no sólo le seguirá proporcionando privacidad, sino que además conseguirá dar más luminosidad, lo que hará que el cuarto de baño parezca más grande. También conseguirá este efecto visual colocando un espejo grande o uno que cubra toda la pared encima del lavabo. Inundar la habitación con luz natural a través de grandes ventanas aumentará también esta sensación de amplitud.

La luz artificial puede utilizarse para iluminar totalmente el cuarto de baño de forma agradable, o puede amortiguarse; en este caso sólo se resaltarían con una fuerte luz los elementos esenciales, como el lavabo o las estanterías. La amplia gama actual de azulejos ofrece la posibilidad de crear interesantes efectos: Las paredes pueden revestirse hasta el techo o sólo hasta el zócalo. Importante es dejar siempre espacio suficiente para guardar los productos de cuarto de baño, de tal forma que no estén a la vista.

La mancanza di spazio è una delle più grandi preoccupazioni quando si progetta il bagno di un appartamento. Se si è a corto di spazi, l'utilizzo di vetro opalino o di mattonelle in vetro per dividere il bagno dalle altre camere garantirà la privacy e contemporaneamente, grazie alla maggiore luminosità, contribuirà a dare l'impressione di un bagno più ampio. Appendendo poi un grande specchio, o meglio ancora coprendo un'intera parete con uno specchio, si otterrà l'effetto ottico di ingrandire ulteriormente gli spazi. Inondando la stanza di luce naturale grazie a grandi finestre, si accrescerà ancor più la sensazione dello spazio. Per creare un ambiente ampio e contemporaneamente caldo, si può ricorrere senza indugio a luci artificiali, oppure le si può anche affievolire e concentrare l'illuminazione nelle zone più importanti quali il lavello o gli scaffali. La vasta offerta odierna di mattonelle consente fantasiose composizioni. Si possono piastrellare le pareti fino al soffitto, oppure si può scegliere una mezza altezza fino allo zoccolo. Per assicurarsi poi sufficienti spazi per gli oggetti, si dovrà cercare di tenere i prodotti da bagno il più possibile in ordine.

Water can be a powerful and poetic force
in the architectural domain, just as it can
in the natural environment.

Al igual que en la naturaleza, en la arquitectura
el agua puede ser una fuerza poética y llena
de energía.

L'acqua possiede una forza dirompente e
poetica, sia nel campo architettonico che
nell'ambiente naturale.

There is something almost monastic about the
ritual of washing. The pleasure of bathing at
the end of a busy day requires an environment
conducive to relaxation and contemplation.

En el ritual de lavarse hay algo casi monacal.
El placer de bañarse después de un día ajetreado
requiere un ambiente que invite a la relajación y
a la contemplación.

C'è qualcosa di profondamente mistico nel rituale
del bagno. Il piacere del bagno alla fine di una
giornata stancante richiede un ambiente
rilassante e che agevoli la meditazione.

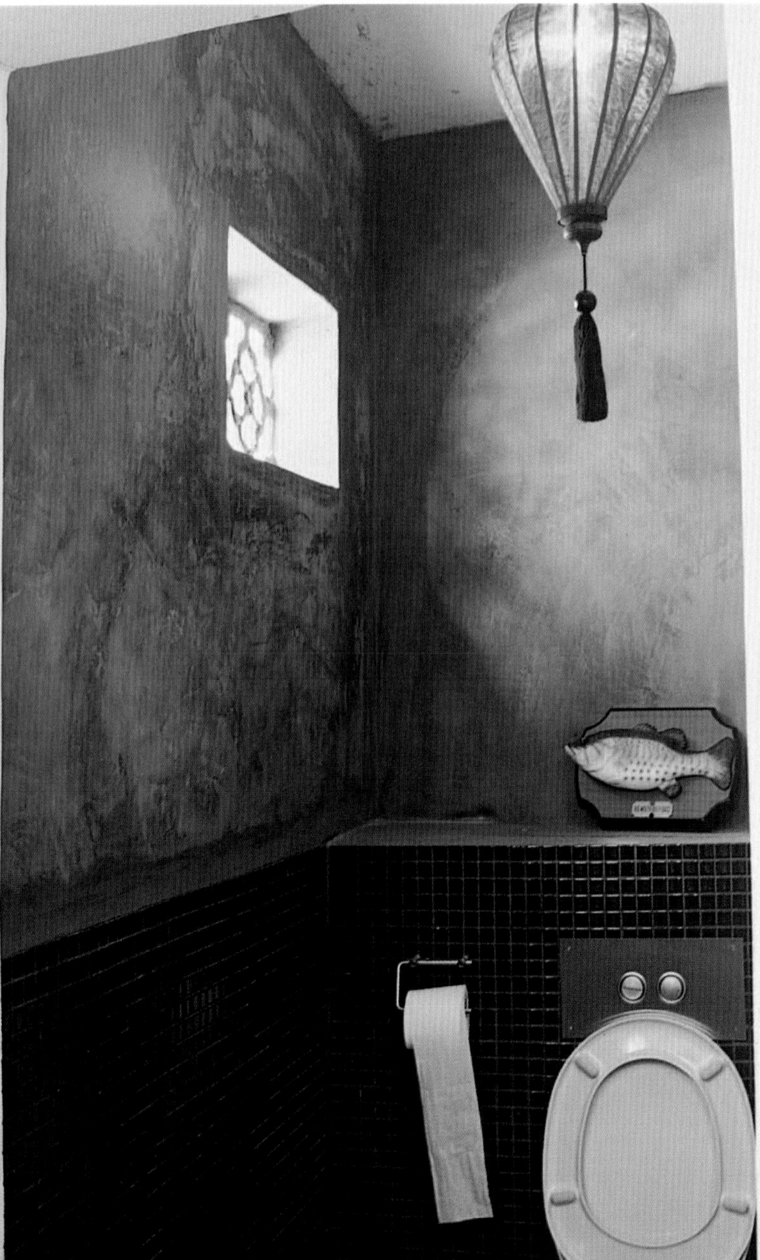

Today's wide selection of tiles offers the potential for interesting textural effects.

La amplia gama actual de azulejos posibilita unos efectos muy interesantes.

La vasta offerta odierna di mattonelle consente fantasiose composizioni.

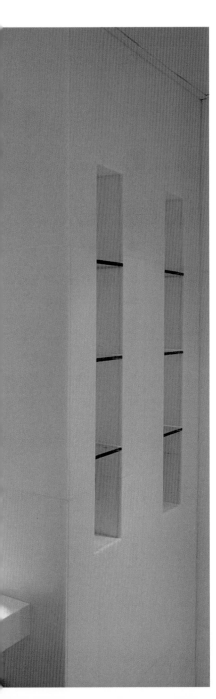

PUNTUATION

openings

Openings are often significantly shaped in Asian architecture, being the important representation of transition between realms of varying levels of publicity and privacy. In tropical areas, extensive openings are integral to vernacular building techniques, having developed, in response to climatic conditions, into a rich means of regional expressions.

INTERRUOPCIÓN

aberturas

Con frecuencia, las aberturas están adaptadas de manera significativa a la arquitectura asiática y constituyen una importante forma de representar la transición entre los distintos niveles de los dominios público y privado. En las zonas tropicales, las amplias aberturas forman parte esencial de las técnicas de construcción autóctonas y, en respuesta a las condiciones climáticas, han acabado convirtiéndose en un fructífero medio de expresión de las particularidades de esas regiones.

INTERRUZIONE

porte e finestre

Porte e finestre sono spesso progettate con molta cura nell'architettura asiatica, rappresentando il passaggio tra i vari livelli di vita pubblica e la sfera privata. Nelle zone tropicali, le grandi vetrate sono parte integrante dell'architettura indigena, evolutasi in armonia con le condizioni climatiche, in una grande varietà di espressioni regionali.

Openings, as well as the level and technique of coverage applied to them, are one of the most important elements of any space. In an apartment, where space may be restricted, a clever choreography and treatment of openings can significantly alter the feeling of spaciousness and quality of light and air flow in your home. Whilst doors and windows physically link spaces and channel the direction of movement, they can also be used as filters that play with spatial flow, overlap, weaving, and penetration.

Openings can either be closed to terminate relationships between spaces or between the interior and exterior, or they can be fully or partially open to create ambiguous relationships. Openings can be orchestrated to manipulate the relationship between private and public, solid and void, feelings of security and vulnerability, shadow and light.

Las aberturas, así como el nivel y la técnica de recubrimiento aplicados, son uno de los elementos más importantes en cualquier espacio. En un apartamento, donde es probable que el espacio esté limitado es posible alterar, de forma significativa, el sentido de amplitud y las condiciones de luz y de ventilación de una vivienda con una ingeniosa coreografía y un inteligente tratamiento de las aberturas. Aunque las puertas y las ventanas unen físicamente los espacios y encauzan la dirección del movimiento, pueden usarse también como filtros para jugar con el flujo, la superposición, el tejido y la penetración en los espacios.

Las aberturas pueden estar cerradas, para cortar las relaciones entre espacios o cortar entre el interior y el exterior, o bien estar total o parcialmente abiertas para crear relaciones ambiguas. Las aberturas pueden organizarse para manipular la relación que se establece entre lo privado y lo público, entre los espacios sólidos y los vacíos, entre los sentimientos de seguridad y los de vulnerabilidad, entre luces y sombras.

Porte e finestre, così come la loro qualità e technica di costruzione, sono uno degli elementi più importanti in qualsiasi spazio abitativo. In un appartamento dalle dimensioni spesso ridotte, una sapiente coreografia e costruzione di porte e finestre può contribuire a modificare la sensazione dello spazio, la qualità dell'illuminazione, oltre che il ricambio dell'aria.

Anche se porte e finestre fisicamente uniscono i vari ambienti e indirizzano gli spostamenti, esse possono anche essere considerate come filtri che giocano con gli spazi, li sovrappongono, li intrecciano, li penetrano.

Porte e finestre si possono tenere chiuse così da definire le relazioni fra i vari spazi della casa o tra quelli interni e quelli esterni, oppure possono essere completamente, o anche solo in parte aperte, creando così relazioni più fluide tra gli spazi. La loro distribuzione nell'appartamento può essere tale da influire sul rapporto tra privato e pubblico, pieno e vuoto, sulla sensazione di sicurezza e di vulnerabilità, tra luce e ombra.

Openings can either be closed to sever relationships between spaces or between the interior and exterior, or they can be fully or partially open to create ambiguous relationships.

Las aberturas pueden estar cerradas, para cortar las relaciones entre espacios o entre el interior y el exterior, o bien estar total o parcialmente abiertas para crear relaciones ambiguas.

Porte e finestre si possono tenere chiuse così da definire le relazioni fra i vari spazi della casa o tra quelli interni e quelli esterni, oppure possono essere completamente, o anche solo in parte aperte, creando così relazioni più fluide tra gli pazi.

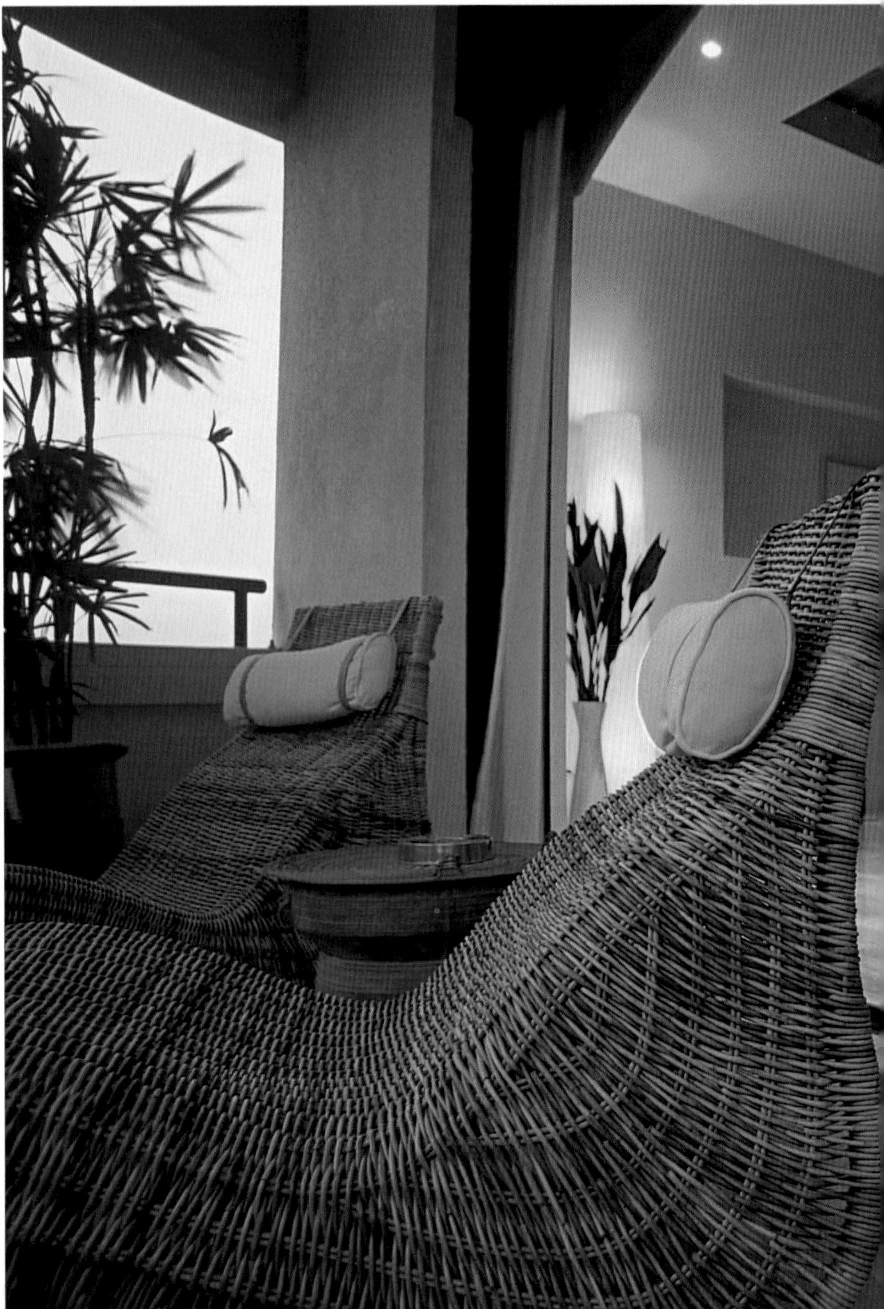

Openings can manipulate the relationship between private and public, solid and void, feelings of security and vulnerability, shadow and light.

Las aberturas pueden organizarse para manipular la relación que se establece entre lo privado y lo público, entre los espacios sólidos y los vacíos, entre los sentimientos de seguridad y los de vulnerabilidad, entre la luz y la sombra.

La loro distribuzione nell'appartamento può essere tale da influire sul rapporto tra privato e pubblico, pieno e vuoto, sulla sensazione di sicurezza e di vulnerabilità, tra luce e ombra.

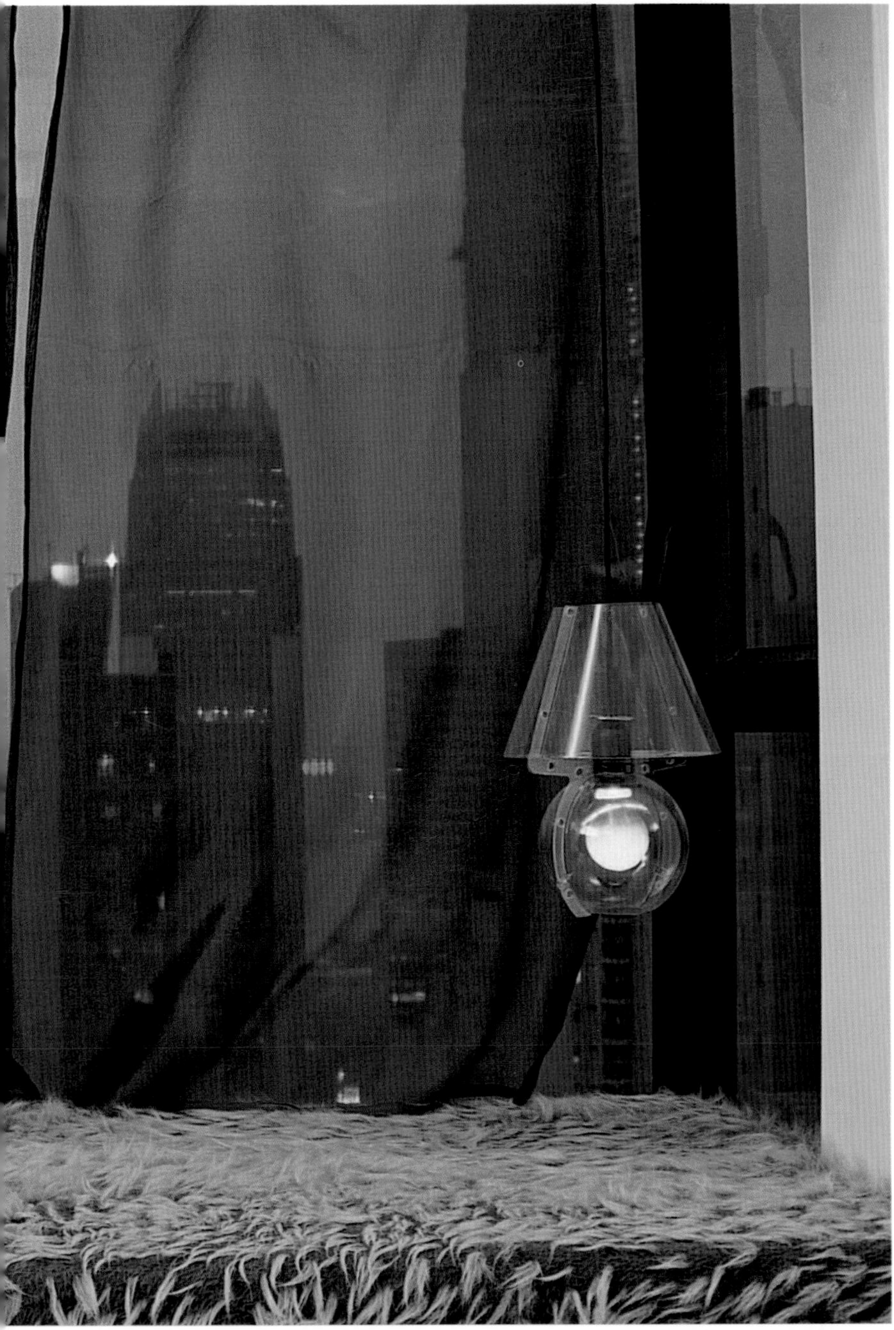

With openings, you can play with spatial flow and overlap, weaving, and penetration.

Por medio de aberturas es posible jugar con el flujo y la superposición de espacios, el tejido y la penetración en los espacios.

Le porte e finestre consentono di giocare con gli spazi, di sovrapporli, intrecciarli e penetrarli.

ILLUMINATION

lighting

In a traditional Asian courtyard house, the intensity of light would vary with the different spaces within the house. The courtyard itself, would of course be bright, and would emit light into surrounding rooms. Corridors, with the sole function of bodily movement, would typically be darker, with less illuminative focuses.

ILUMINACIÓN

luz

En las casas tradicionales asiáticas con jardines interiores, la intensidad de la luz variaba en los diferentes espacios del interior de la vivienda. Como es lógico, el patio era luminoso y proporcionaba luz a las habitaciones de alrededor. Los pasillos, con una única función de paso, solían ser oscuros, con menos focos de luz.

ILLUMINAZIONE

luce

Nella tradizionale casa con cortile asiatica l'intensità della luce cambia notevolmente a seconda delle stanze. Il cortile stesso sarà naturalmente luminoso e trasmetterà luce anche alle camere che lo circondano. I corridoi, con la loro unica funzione di passaggio, sono tipicamente più bui e hanno meno punti illuminati.

Whilst light itself is ethereal and intangible, dimensionless and unable to be touched, it is perhaps the defining element of any space. Without light, after all, we would not even be able to see space. The lighting of a space can influence its perceived size, its mood – dreamy, intense, warm, cool, intimate, sterile, soft, hard – and can be suggestive of its function. For example, spaces for work require bright, focused light, while spaces for relaxation can be dimly illuminated.

The planning of the artificial lighting for your apartment requires, first of all, a consideration of the natural lighting conditions. Consider the natural light quality of the area in which you live, and the strength of the light at different times of the day and year. This will help you to determine the amount of artificial light needed during the day, and whether this differs from the amount needed at night.

Aunque en sí la luz es etérea e intangible, carece de dimensiones y no se puede tocar, es quizás el elemento más decisivo en cualquier espacio. Al fin y al cabo, sin la luz no seríamos capaces ni de ver el espacio. La iluminación de una estancia puede influir en la percepción de su tamaño, así como en su atmósfera —soñadora, intensa, cálida, fresca, íntima, yerma, suave, dura— y puede hacer pensar en su función. Así por ejemplo, los espacios de trabajo necesitan luz brillante y enfocada, mientras que en los destinados al descanso basta con una luz tenue.

Al planificar la iluminación artificial de su apartamento es necesario antes que nada tener en cuenta las condiciones de luz natural. Considere las cualidades de la luz natural de la zona en la que vive, y la intensidad de la luz a las diferentes horas del día y en las distintas épocas del año. Esto le ayudará a determinar la cantidad de luz artificial necesaria durante el día, y si varía con respecto a la cantidad que es necesaria de noche.

Anche se la luce in sé è un elemento etereo e intangibile, inconsistente e impalpabile, è pur tuttavia l'elemento indispensabile per la definizione di qualsiasi spazio. L'illuminazione può trasformare la percezione che si ha della grandezza degli spazi e la loro atmosfera, che sia languida, intensa, calda o fredda, intima, sterile, soffice o dura, e la sua distribuzione viene naturalmente definita dalla funzione a cui gli spazi sono adibiti. Una stanza in cui si lavora deve essere luminosa con punti di luce ben definiti, mentre le stanze in cui ci si rilassa possono avere un' illuminazione più soffusa.

Per pianificare l'illuminazione artificiale di un appartamento bisogna tenere conto in primo luogo delle condizioni di luce naturale. È necessario considerarne la qualità nella zona in cui si abita e l'intensità nei diversi momenti della giornata nonché dell'anno. Questa analisi consentirà di stabilire di quanta luce artificiale si ha bisogno durante il giorno e di quanta di notte.

Light fittings can produce a myriad of light effects.

Por medio de complementos de iluminación pueden lograrse un sinfín de efectos luminosos.

Con una distribuzione studiata dell'illuminazione si possono creare svariati effetti di luce.

Light itself is ethereal and intangible,
dimensionless and unable to be touched, yet it is
perhaps the defining element of any space.

En sí la luz es etérea e intangible, carece de
dimensiones y no se puede tocar, pero es quizás el
elemento más decisivo en cualquier espacio.

Anche se la luce in sé è un elemento etereo
e intangibile, inconsistente e impalpabile, è pur
tuttavia l'elemento indispensabile per la
definizione di qualsiasi spazio.

The planning of the artificial lighting for your apartment requires first of all a consideration of the natural lighting conditions.

Al planificar la iluminación artificial de su apartamento es necesario antes que nada tener en cuenta las condiciones de luz natural.

Per pianificare l'illuminazione artificiale di un appartamento bisogna tenere conto in primo luogo delle condizioni di luce naturale.

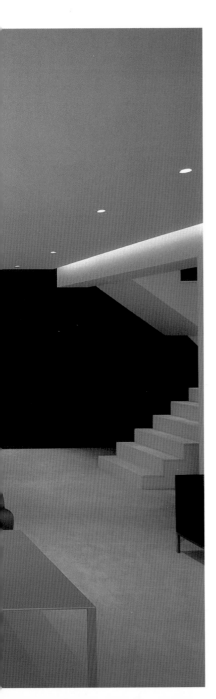

COMPOSITION

colours

Inspired by natural materials and landscapes, the Asian colour palette is composed primarily of the soothing shades of the earth – browns, creams and whites are the base colours, punctuated perhaps by a bold red or another colour associated with tradition or religion.

COMPOSICIÓN

colores

Inspirada en materiales y paisajes naturales, la paleta de colores asiática está compuesta primordialmente por los relajantes tonos sombra de la tierra: los marrones, los cremas y los blancos son los colores base, realzados si acaso por un rojo vivo u otro color asociado a la tradición o la religión.

COMPOSIZIONE

colore

La tavolozza dei colori asiatici, ispirata a materiali e paesaggi naturali, è composta essenzialmente dalle riposanti sfumature della terra: marrone, beige e bianco sono i colori base, ravvivati forse a volte da un rosso acceso o da un altro colore associato a contenuti tradizionali o religiosi.

Colour is a powerful element in design. A single, colorful object in a neutral room will immediately draw the attention of the eye, and everything else will recede into the background. Light is, of course, the element that facilitates our perception of colour, but experts in the field of colour theory argue that colour is not just seen – it is also felt emotionally. Indeed, individuals do tend to resonate towards different colours. Particular interpretations of colour mean that the choice of a colour scheme for your apartment is a very personal matter. Begin your process of colour selection by choosing colours that move you. When choosing colours, hold up swatches around the room at various times of the day and under artificial light. Colours can be transformed by different light conditions, and seasonal difference also has a great impact on colour.

El color es un poderoso elemento en el diseño. Un único objeto de color vivo en una habitación neutra atraerá en seguida la atención de la vista, y todo lo demás quedará en un segundo plano. La luz es, por supuesto, el elemento que facilita nuestra percepción del color, pero los expertos en el ámbito de la teoría de los colores argumentan que el color no sólo se ve, sino que además provoca una respuesta emocional. En efecto, los individuos tienden a reaccionar ante determinados colores. Teniendo en cuenta las interpretaciones particulares que se le da al color, la selección de un esquema cromático para su apartamento es una cuestión muy personal. Inicie el proceso de selección del color eligiendo aquellos que le susciten alguna emoción.

Al seleccionar los colores, camine por la habitación sosteniendo muestras de un color a diferentes horas del día, y con luz artificial. Los colores pueden transformarse según las distintas condiciones de iluminación, y la diferencia de estaciones también puede tener un gran impacto en el color.

Il colore è un elemento assai efficace nel design di interni. Un unico oggetto colorato in una stanza altrimenti priva di particolarità, cattura subito l'attenzione confinando tutto il resto su un piano di importanza secondario. La luce facilita naturalmente la nostra percezione del colore e i teorici del colore arrivano addirittura a dire che esso non ha solo a che fare con la vista, ma che è in grado di influenzare le nostre emozioni. Inoltre le particolarità degli oggetti vengono valorizzate diversamente a seconda dei colori. L'interpretazione che ognuno di noi dà di un colore implica che la scelta che se ne fa per il proprio appartamento sia sempre soggettiva; la scelta parte dai colori che riescono in qualche modo a dirci qualcosa.

Una volta scelti i colori bisognerà poi fare alcune prove nei vari punti della stanza, con luce naturale in ore diverse, ma anche con luce artificiale. I colori si trasformano in base alle condizioni di luce e anche le stagioni modificano enormemente la loro percezione.

Begin your process of colour selection by choosing colours that move you.

Inicie la selección del color eligiendo los colores que le susciten alguna emoción.

La scelta deve partire da quei colori che riescono in qualche modo a dirci qualcosa.

Particular interpretations of colour mean that the choice of a colour scheme for your apartment is a very personal matter.

Teniendo en cuenta las interpretaciones particulares que se le da al color, la selección de un esquema cromático para su apartamento es una cuestión muy personal.

L'interpretazione che ognuno di noi dà di un colore implica che la scelta che se ne fa per il proprio appartamento sia sempre soggettiva.

Colour can be manipulated to alter the perceived size and spatial conception of a room.

El color puede manipularse para alterar la percepción del tamaño y la concepción espacial de una habitación.

I colori possono essere utilizzati per modificare la percezione spaziale che si ha di una stanza.

ACCENTUATION

textures and fabrics

Traditional Asian architecture has typically had an air of sensuality about it. Its palette of natural materials such as timber, rattan, bamboo and stone, and its delicate articulation of joints, have given it an attractive dimension that is palpable to the human scale and touch.

ACENTUACIÓN

texturas y tejidos

La arquitectura asiática tradicional siempre se ha caracterizado por un aire de sensualidad. Su gama de materiales naturales, como la madera, la rota, el bambú y la piedra, y su delicada forma de articular las uniones, le han proporcionado una dimensión atractiva en la que quedan patentes las proporciones y el calor humanos.

ACCENTO

materiale e struttura

La tradizionale architettura asiatica è permeata da un'aurea di sensualità. La grande varietà di materiali naturali utilizzati, quali legno, rattan, bambù e pietra e le loro delicate combinazioni la rendono piacevole sia da un punto di vista visivo che tattile.

Textures and fabrics can ease the hardness of the solid planes and volumes, which are characteristic of contemporary designs, and create an interesting layering effect at the same time. Texture can be two- or three-dimensional and whilst two-dimensional surface texture consists of patterns, three-dimensional texture has a depth that is revealed through light and shadow. Two-dimensional textures are best on walls, and for floors that must sustain a high level of traffic. The natural patterns in stone can produce beautiful compositions on the wall or floor when tiles cut from the same rock are aligned side by side. Timber floorboards of various widths and lengths, parquetry, cork, carpets, polished concrete and ceramic tiles of various colours and levels of finish can all create satisfying two-dimensional textures. Three-dimensional textures are best appreciated at places where the body lingers, such as the bed, lounge, or on a feature rug in the living room for example. Visual features can also be made of three-dimensional textures, such as, a wall clad in roughly hewn stone or a roughly plastered wall. These surfaces can be visually sumptuous when the textural depth is sufficiently highlighted by light. Light itself can also produce compelling textures composed of a play of light and shadow.

Por medio de texturas y tejidos se puede suavizar la dureza de los planos y volúmenes sólidos, tan característicos de los diseños contemporáneos, y crear al mismo tiempo un interesante efecto de superposición. La textura puede ser bidimensional o tridimensional: mientras que la textura bidimensional está formada por dibujos, la textura tridimensional tiene una profundidad que se revela por medio de luces y sombras. Las texturas bidimensionales resultan idóneas para paredes y para suelos expuestos a un tránsito frecuente. Con motivos naturales esculpidos en piedra pueden lograrse bellas composiciones en la pared o en el suelo alineando baldosas fabricadas a partir de esa misma piedra. Por medio de suelos de madera de distintos anchos y longitudes, parquet, corcho, alfombras, hormigón pulido y baldosas de cerámica de diferentes colores y niveles de acabado pueden crearse texturas bidimensionales satisfactorias.

Las texturas tridimensionales se aprecian mejor en los espacios destinados al descanso, como por ejemplo en la cama, en la sala de estar o en una alfombra central en el salón. Los rasgos visuales pueden lograrse también con texturas tridimensionales, por ejemplo con un revestimiento de paredes en piedra toscamente labrada o una pared toscamente enyesada. Con estas superficies pueden conseguirse efectos visuales suntuosos si la profundidad de la textura está suficientemente resaltada por la luz. Por sí misma, la luz es también capaz de producir atractivas texturas a partir de un juego de luces y sombras.

Materiali e strutture possono attenuare la rigidità dei piani e volumi uniformi caratteristici del moderno design, creando al tempo stesso un interessante effetto compositivo. Si possono creare strutture a due o tre dimensioni; mentre le superfici composte bidimensionalmente sono più che altro disegni e decorazioni piane, quelle tridimensionali hanno una profondità che viene esaltata dai giochi di luce e ombra. Strutture bidimensionali sono perfette alle pareti o per i pavimenti che devono sopportare un gran via vai. Un disegno naturale in pietra può rivelarsi una splendida composizione, sistemando le mattonelle, provenienti dalla stessa roccia, una accanto all'altra. Tavole di legno di diversa larghezza e lunghezza, parquet, sughero, tappeti, cemento lucido, e mattonelle di ceramica di diversi colori e gradi di rifinitura, sono tutti materiali perfetti per creare bellissime composizioni bidimensionali. Le creazioni tridimensionali sono più appropriate in quei luoghi in cui ci si intrattiene fisicamente, come il letto, il soggiorno, o una zona decorata con tappeti particolari. Molto interessanti da vedere, le creazioni a struttura tridimensionale si possono utilizzare per le pareti, ricoprendole ad esempio con pietre tagliate in modo irregolare o intonacandole in modo grezzo. Sono superfici che possono risultare addirittura sfarzose nel momento in cui la luce metta in risalto i diversi livelli di materiale. I giochi stessi di luce e ombra possono creare composizioni straordinarie.

Textures and fabrics can create an interesting layering effect.

Por medio de texturas y de tejidos puede crear un interesante efecto de superposición.

Materiali e strutture possono creare un interessante effetto compositivo.

You can retain a simple aesthetic while inserting textures and fabrics to capture the eye, stimulate the sense of touch, and feed the soul.

Es posible lograr un sencillo efecto estético insertando texturas y tejidos que atraen la vista, estimulan el sentido del tacto y alimentan el espíritu.

Si può conservare la bellezza semplice degli ambienti utilizzando materiali e composizioni che catturano lo sguardo, stimolano il tatto e sono un balsamo per l'anima.

we are

the artwork of god

EXPRESSION

art and sculpture

Art and sculpture in traditional Asian housing is typically connected to religious or ancient wisdoms. In a Chinese house, for example, art is instructional to a certain degree – speaking of myths, morals and values, with an emphasis on the concept of family and religion.

EXPRESIÓN

arte y escultura

En la vivienda asiática, es típico que el arte y la escultura estén relacionados con creencias religiosas o ancestrales. En las casas chinas, por ejemplo, el arte es en cierto modo educativo: en él se habla de mitos, moralejas y valores, haciendo énfasis en el concepto de familia y de religión.

ESPRESSIONE

arte e scultura

L'arte e la scultura nelle abitazioni asiatiche sono tradizionalmente legate alla religione e alla saggezza antiche. Nelle case cinesi l'arte ha un valore anche didattico e racconta di miti, morale e valori, evidenziando soprattutto concetti quali la famiglia e la religione.

Art and sculpture with which we choose to adorn our homes is an expression of our own desires and tastes. It is soul food that tells us about the past and the future, as our perceptions of it change with time. Art and sculpture can add exciting visual and conceptual dimensions to the domestic interior.

Like a sub-plot in interior design, art and sculpture can be an important apparatus in the emphasis and reinforcement of the design concept. Instead of perceiving art and sculpture as mere decorative objects, these pieces can be arranged to complement the space visually and conceptually. In addition, art can easily be a conversation piece; it enlivens any space, and tells stories of both the space and the person behind the space.

El arte y la escultura que elegimos para decorar nuestros hogares es una expresión de nuestros deseos y gustos. Es alimento para el espíritu que nos informa acerca del pasado y del futuro, dado que nuestras percepciones cambian con el tiempo. El arte y la escultura pueden añadir atractivas dimensiones visuales y conceptuales al interior del hogar. A modo de argumento secundario en el diseño de interiores, el arte y la escultura pueden ser una importante herramienta a la hora de lograr el énfasis y el refuerzo del concepto de diseño. En vez de percibir el arte y la escultura como meros objetos decorativos, estas piezas pueden disponerse de forma que complementen el espacio visual y conceptualmente.

Asimismo el arte puede convertirse fácilmente en un motivo de conversación; da vida a cualquier espacio, y nos dice mucho tanto del espacio como de la persona que hay detrás de él.

L'arte e la scultura con cui adorniamo la nostra casa sono la diretta espressione dei nostri desideri e dei nostri gusti. Sono alimento per lo spirito e ci raccontano del passato e del futuro, facendoci percepire la loro metamorfosi nel tempo e aggiungendo scorci visivi interessanti e nuove dimensioni concettuali tra le pareti domestiche.

Secondarie nel design di interni, in realtà arte e scultura possono fornire interessanti soluzioni per enfatizzare e rafforzare il concetto stesso di design. Invece di considerare gli oggetti artistici e i pezzi di scultura quali mere decorazioni, essi possono essere disposti nella casa a complemento dello spazio visuale nonché concettuale. L'arte oltretutto può facilmente essere oggetto di conversazione; anima lo spazio e racconta storie che riguardano sia lo spazio che le persone che lo abitano.

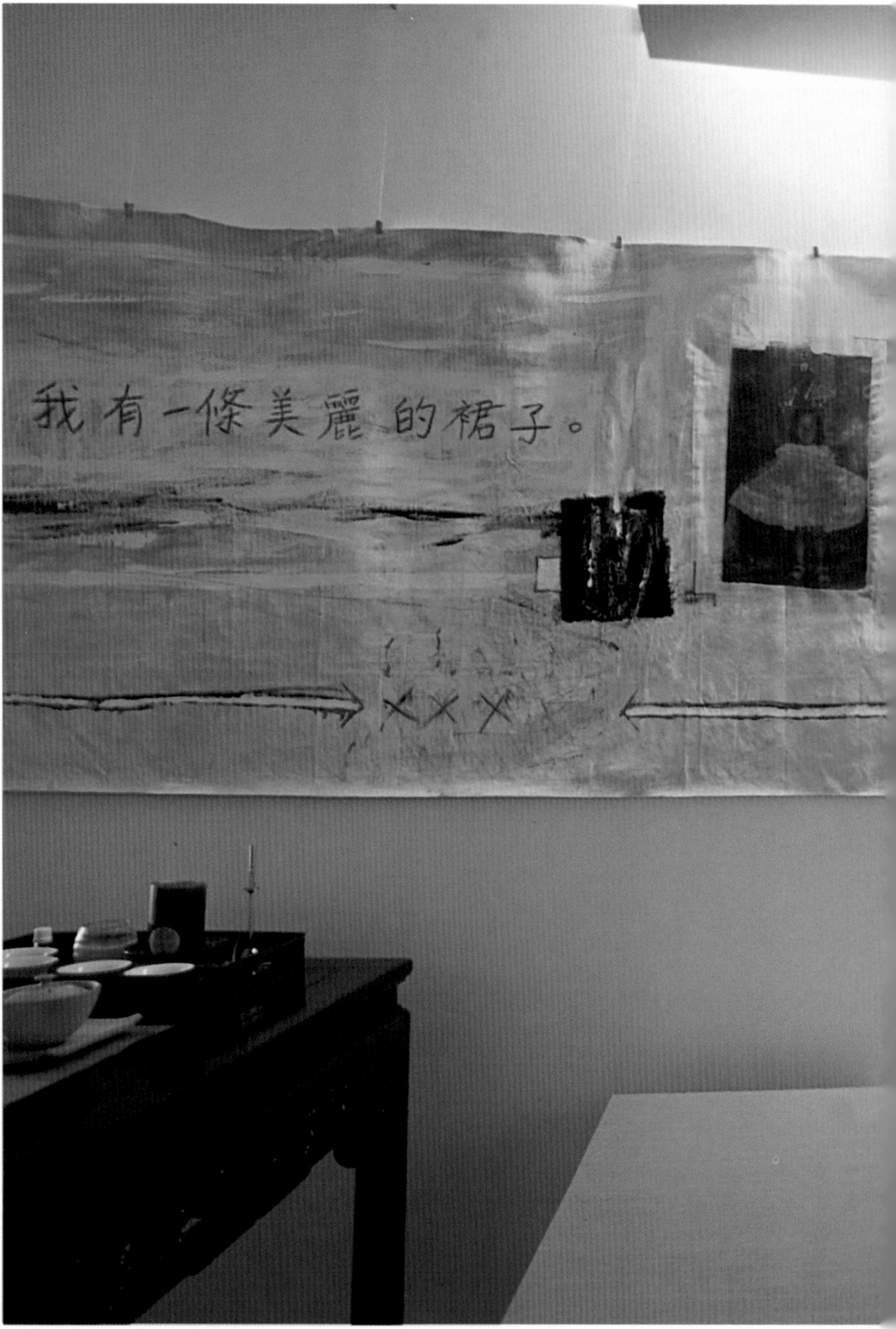
我有一條美麗的裙子。

Art and sculpture can add an exciting visual and
conceptual dimension to the domestic interior.

El arte y la escultura pueden añadir una atractiva
dimensión visual y conceptual al interior del hogar.

L'arte e la scultura aggiungono scorci visivi
interessanti e nuove dimensioni concettuali tra
le pareti domestiche.

SURGERY IN PROGRESS

Like a sub-plot to the interior design, art and sculpture can be an important apparatus in the emphasis and reinforcement of the design concept.

A modo de argumento secundario en el diseño de interiores, el arte y la escultura pueden ser una importante herramienta a la hora de lograr el énfasis y el refuerzo del concepto de diseño.

Secondarie nel design di interni, in realtà arte e scultura possono fornire interessanti soluzioni per enfatizzare e rafforzare il concetto stesso di design.

INTEGRATION

decorative accessories

Asian interiors are, generally, neither decorated flamboyantly nor extravagantly. Often a furniture of a heavily detailed composition has performed a dual function of utility and decoration.

INTEGRACIÓN

accesorios decorativos

Por lo general, en Asia la decoración de interiores no suele ser ni recargada ni extravagante. A menudo, el mobiliario de una composición con excesivos detalles ha desempeñado una doble función utilitaria y decorativa.

INTEGRAZIONE

accessori decorativi

Le abitazioni asiatiche non sono generalmente decorate in modo sgargiante e stravagante. Spesso l'arredamento, dalla composizione pesantemente dettagliata, adempie a due funzioni, è cioè utile e decorativo.

Decorative accessorising need not be excessive. Often, restraint can speak louder than careless adornment. Accessorising need only be succinct, like poetry, and suitable to the rest of the interior. A single object of adornment is often sufficient to imbue a space with a great deal of depth and interest. Good accessorising can tie up the loose ends of a design scheme, as well as enrich and reinforce the character of the space. Accessories can describe a theme or story – they can add another layer of meaning to an interior. Harnessing the decorative potential of simple objects can be a terrific way to enliven your apartment if you are unable to afford the luxury of fine art.

No es necesario abusar en el empleo de accesorios decorativos. Con frecuencia, la sobriedad puede producir más impacto que el uso de adornos sin ton ni son. Ante todo, los accesorios deben ser sucintos, como la poesía, y no desentonar con el resto del interior de la vivienda. Un único objeto decorativo basta a menudo para imbuir a un espacio de una gran profundidad e interés. Un empleo adecuado de los accesorios puede servir para atar los cabos sueltos de un esquema de diseño, así como para enriquecer y reforzar el carácter de un espacio. Los accesorios pueden describir un tema o una historia, añadir un nuevo matiz de significado al interior de una vivienda.
Aprovechar el potencial decorativo de objetos sencillos puede ser un modo estupendo de dar vida a su apartamento si el lujo de las bellas artes no se encuentra a su alcance.

Gli accessori decorativi non devono essere esagerati. Spesso ornamenti delicati dicono molto di più che pacchianate senza garbo. Gli accessori devono semplicemente essere "brevi", come una poesia, e adattarsi al resto della casa. Un singolo oggetto ornamentale è spesso sufficiente per trasmettere all'intero ambiente un particolare significato e interesse. Accessori ben scelti possono completare un design di interni a cui mancava qualcosa, oltre che arricchire e rinvigorire gli spazi. Gli accessori possono raccontare una storia o descrivere un tema, possono arricchire di significati l'arredamento. Evidenziare il potenziale decorativo dei singoli oggetti è uno dei modi migliori per vivacizzare un appartamento quando non ci si può permettere il lusso dell'arte.

Decorative accessorising need not be excessive. Often restraint can speak louder than profusion.

No es necesario abusar en el empleo de accesorios decorativos. Con frecuencia, la sobriedad puede producir más impacto que la profusión.

Gli accessori decorativi non devono essere esagerati. Spesso ornamenti delicati dicono molto di più che pacchianate senza garbo.

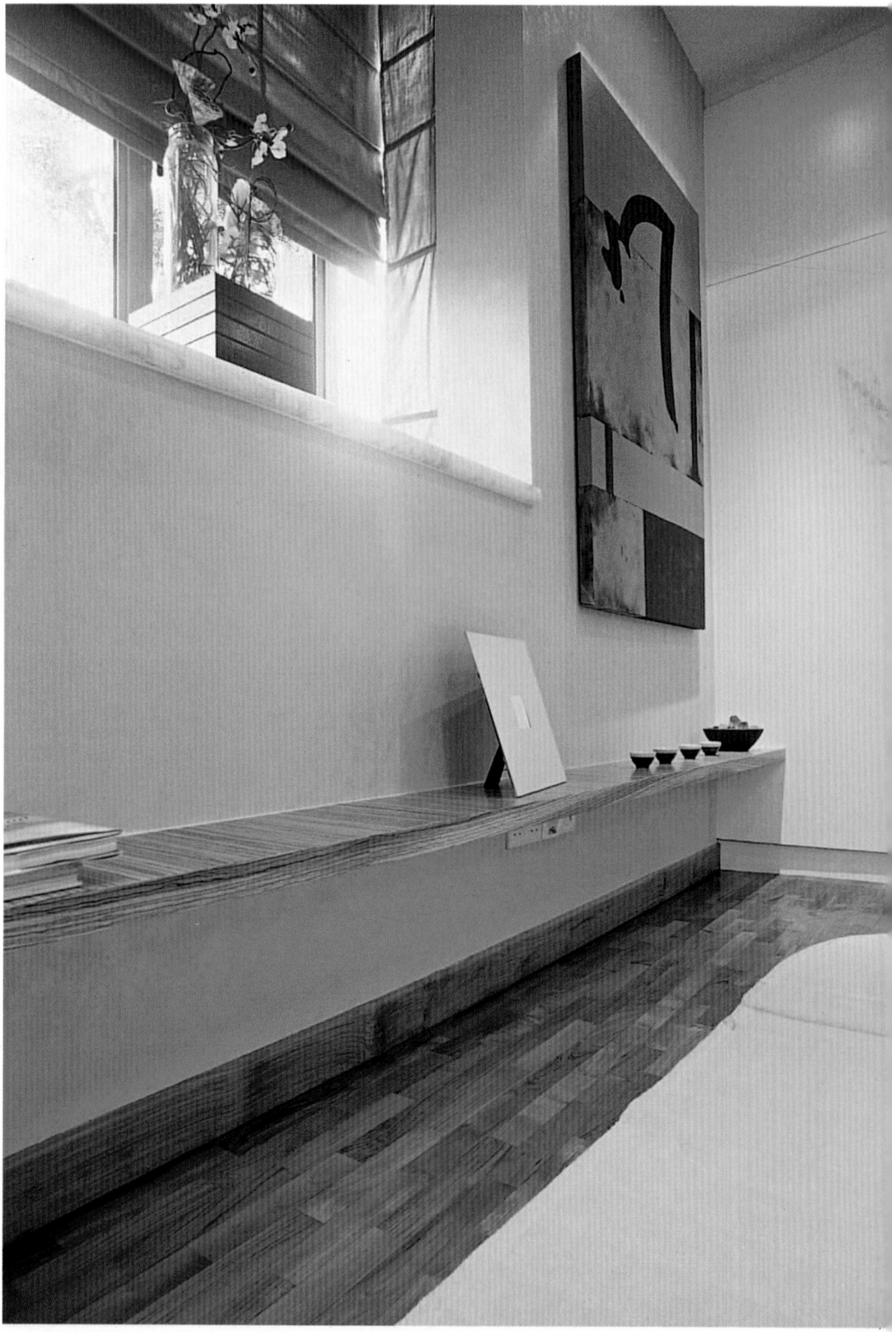

Accessorising need only be succinct, like poetry, and suitable to the rest of the interior.

Ante todo, los accesorios deben de ser sucintos, como la poesía, y no desentonar con el resto del interior de la vivienda.

Gli accessori devono semplicemente essere brevi, come una poesia, e adattarsi al resto della casa.

photo credits
créditos fotográficos
crediti fotografici

Key: **l** = left, **r** = right, **t** = top, **b** = bottom

Photography by Kelley Cheng unless otherwise stated.

Vestibules and Corridors 9 Designed by Index Design Pte Ltd (Singapore); Photography by Tan Kah Heng/Courtesy of *ish* (Singapore) **11** Designed by Warren Liu and Darlene Smyth (Singapore); Photography by Rida Sobana/Courtesy of Warren Liu **13** Designed by Cu Fua Associates (Singapore) **14-15** Designed by Cu Fua Associates (Singapore) **16-17** Designed by Dillon Garis Design Solutions (Hong Kong) **18** Designed by Whiz Concepts (Singapore) **19** Designed by Whiz Concepts (Singapore) **20-21** Designed by Terence Chan/TREE (Singapore) **22** Designed by Whiz Concepts (Singapore) **23** Designed by Albano Daminato Studio (Singapore) **24-25** Designed by Whiz Concepts (Singapore) **26-27** Designed by Joey Ho (Singapore) **28** Designed by Tony Chan/CREAM Design + Architectural Planning (Hong Kong); Photography courtesy of Tony Chan/CREAM Design + Architectural Planning (Hong Kong) **29** Designed by Alexander Wong/Asiacity Ltd (Hong Kong) **30** Designed by Marcel Heijnen (Singapore) **31** Designed by Rene Tan (Singapore) **Living Rooms 33-35** Designed by Index Design Pte Ltd (Singapore); Photography by Tan Kah Heng/Courtesy of *ish* (Singapore) **37** Designed by Whiz Concepts (Singapore) **38-39** Designed by Wide Open Spaces (Singapore) **40** Designed by Whiz Concepts (Singapore) **41** Designed by Alexander Wong/Asiacity Ltd (Hong Kong) **42-43** Designed by Tony Chan/CREAM Design + Architectural Planning (Hong Kong); Photography courtesy of Tony Chan/CREAM Design + Architectural Planning (Hong Kong) **44-45** Designed by Terence Chan/TREE (Singapore) **46** Designed by Alexander Wong/Asiacity Ltd (Hong Kong) **47** Designed by Terence Chan/TREE (Singapore) **48** Designed by Pichai-Theeranuj Wongwaisayawan (Bangkok) **49** Designed by Rene Tan (Singapore) **50-51** Designed by Cu Fua Associates (Singapore) **52-53** Designed by Cu Fua Associates (Singapore) **54-55** Designed by K2LD Architects (Singapore) **56-57** Designed by Cynosure Design Associates (Singapore) **58-59** Designed by Cu Fua Associates (Singapore) **60-61** Designed by Albano Daminato Studio (Singapore) **62-63** Designed by Terence Chan/TREE (Singapore) **64-65** Designed by Cu Fua Associates (Singapore) **66** Designed by Thor (Singapore) **67** Designed by Room Interior Pte Ltd (Singapore) **68-69** Designed by Room Interior Pte Ltd (Singapore) **70-71** Designed by Draughtzman (Hong Kong) **72** Designed

(Singapore); Photography by Sonny Sandjaya/Courtesy of K2LD Architects (Singapore) **204** Designed by Pichai-Theeranuj Wongwaisayawan (Bangkok) **205** Designed by Dillon Garis Design Solutions (Hong Kong) **206-207** Designed by The Matchbox (Singapore) **208-209** Designed by Alexander Wong/Asiacity Ltd (Hong Kong) **210** Designed by Whiz Concepts (Singapore) **211** Designed by Wide Open Spaces (Singapore) **212** Designed by Brenda Ng/Weave Interior (Singapore) **213** Designed by Brenda Ng/Weave Interior (Singapore) **214-215** Designed by Alexander Wong/Asiacity Ltd (Hong Kong) **216-219** Designed by Marcel Heijnen and Hund & Pups (Singapore) **220(l)** Designed by Brenda Ng/Weave Interior (Singapore) **220(r)** Designed by Pichai-Theeranuj Wongwaisayawan (Bangkok) **221** Designed by KNTA Architects (Singapore); Photography by CI&A Photography/Courtesy of *ish* (Singapore) **222-223** Designed by Tony Chan/CREAM Design + Architectural Planning (Hong Kong); Photography courtesy of Tony Chan/CREAM Design + Architectural Planning (Hong Kong) **224-225(tl-tr)** Designed by Terence Chan/TREE (Singapore) **225(b)** Designed by Brenda Ng/Weave Interior (Singapore) **226** Designed by Alexander Wong/Asiacity Ltd (Hong Kong) **227** Designed by A+P Regional (Singapore) **Openings 229** Designed by Joey Ho (Singapore) **231** Designed by Tony Chan/CREAM Design + Architectural Planning (Hong Kong); Photography courtesy of Tony Chan/CREAM Design + Architectural Planning (Hong Kong) **233-239** Designed by Alexander Wong/Asiacity Ltd (Hong Kong) **240-241** Designed by Pichai-Theeranuj Wongwaisayawan (Bangkok) **242-243** Designed by Marcel Heijnen (Singapore) **244-247** Designed by Cu Fua Associates (Singapore) **248** Designed by Marcel Heijnen (Singapore) **249** Designed by Rene Tan (Singapore) **250-251** Designed by Draughtzman (Hong Kong) **252-253** Designed by Whiz Concepts (Singapore) **254** Designed by Harry & Carrie and Hund & Pups (Singapore) **255** Designed by Whiz Concepts (Singapore) **256-257** Designed by Terence Chan/TREE (Singapore) **258** Designed by Warren Liu and Darlene Smyth (Singapore); Photography by Rida Sobana/Courtesy of Warren Liu **259** Designed by Rene Tan (Singapore) **260-261** Designed by Wide Open Spaces CREAM (Singapore) **Lighting 263** Designed by Joey Ho (Singapore) **265** Designed by Cu Fua Associates (Singapore) **271** Designed by Warren Liu and Darlene Smyth (Singapore) **268-269** Designed by Joey Ho (Singapore) **270** Designed by Cu Fua Associates (Singapore) **272-273** Designed by K2LD Architects (Singapore) **274-275** Designed by Whiz Concepts (Singapore); Photography by Rida Sobana/Courtesy of Warren Liu **272-273** Designed by K2LD Architects (Singapore) **278-279** Designed by Cynosure Design Associates (Singapore) **280-281** Designed by (Singapore) **276-277** Designed by Cu Fua Associates (Singapore) **283** Designed by Whiz Concepts (Singapore) **284-285** Designed by Terence Chan/TREE Joey Ho (Singapore) **282** Designed by Draughtzman (Hong Kong)

(Singapore) **286** Designed by Whiz Concepts (Singapore) **287** Designed by K2LD Architects (Singapore) **288-289** Designed by ARC STUDIO and Spacecraft (Singapore) **290** Designed by A+P Regional (Singapore) **291** Designed by Cynosure Design Associates (Singapore) **292** Designed by Rene Tan (Singapore) **293** Designed by OM Home (Singapore); Photography courtesy of *ish* (Singapore) **294-297** Designed by Tony Chan/CREAM Design + Architectural Planning (Hong Kong); Photography courtesy of Tony Chan/CREAM Design + Architectural Planning (Hong Kong) **Colours 299** Designed by OM Home (Singapore); Photography courtesy of *ish* (Singapore) **301** Designed by CREAM (Singapore) **303** Designed by Kelly Lee (Singapore) **304** Designed by OM Home (Singapore); Photography courtesy of *ish* (Singapore) **305** Designed by Rene Tan (Singapore) **306-307** Designed by KNTA Architects (Singapore); Photography by CI&A Photography/Courtesy of *ish* (Singapore) **308-309** Designed by K2LD Architects (Singapore) **310** Designed by TRAX (Singapore); Photography courtesy of *ish* (Singapore) **311-313** Designed by K2LD Architects (Singapore); Photography by Sonny Sandjaya/Courtesy of K2LD Architects (Singapore) **314** Designed by Wallflower Architecture and Design (Singapore) **315** Designed by James and Grace Tan (Singapore) **316-317** Designed by Rene Tan (Singapore) **318** Designed by Draughtzman (Hong Kong) **319** Designed by Kelly Lee (Singapore) **Textures and Fabrics 321-323** Designed by Cu Fua Associates (Singapore) **325-327** Designed by MOIE (Singapore) **328** Designed by Cynosure Design Associates (Singapore) **329** Designed by Cu Fua Associates (Singapore) **330** Designed by Pichai-Theeranuj Wongwaisayawan (Bangkok) **331** Designed by Warren Liu and Darlene Smyth (Singapore); Photography by Rida Sobana/Courtesy of Warren Liu **332-333** Designed by Cynosure Design Associates (Singapore) **334-335** Designed by K2LD Architects (Singapore); Photography by Sonny Sandjaya/Courtesy of K2LD Architects (Singapore) **336** Designed by Kelly Lee (Singapore) **337** Designed by Terence Chan/TREE (Singapore) **338-339** Designed by Joey Ho (Singapore) **340** Designed by Thor (Singapore) **341** Designed by Draughtzman (Hong Kong) **Art and Sculpture 343** Designed by Peter Tay (Singapore); Photography by Geoff Ang/Courtesy of *ish* (Singapore) **345** Designed by OM Home (Singapore); Photography courtesy of *ish* (Singapore) **347** Designed by Rene Tan (Singapore) **348-349** Designed by Draughtzman (Hong Kong) **350** Designed by K2LD Architects (Singapore) **351** Designed by Kelly Lee (Singapore) **352-355** Designed by Joey Ho (Singapore) **356** Designed by Whiz Concepts (Singapore) **357** Designed by Albano Daminato Studio (Singapore) **358-359** Designed by Terence Chan/TREE (Singapore) **360-361** Designed by Cu Fua Associates (Singapore) **362** Designed by Room Interior Pte Ltd (Singapore) **363** Designed by Rene Tan (Singapore) **364-365** Designed by Cynosure Design Associates (Singapore) **Decorative Accessories 367** Designed by Joey Ho (Singapore) **369** Designed by Rene Tan (Singapore) **370-371** Designed by TRAX (Singapore); Photography courtesy of *ish* (Singapore) **372** Designed by Kelly Lee (Singapore) **373** Designed by Whiz Concepts (Singapore) **374** Designed by K2LD Architects (Singapore) **375** Designed by Zong Architects (Singapore) **376** Designed by Cynosure Design Associates (Singapore) **377** Designed by Pichai-Theeranuj Wongwaisayawan (Bangkok) **378-381** Designed by Marcel Heijnen (Singapore) **382** Designed by OM Home (Singapore); Photography courtesy of *ish* (Singapore) **383** Designed by MOIE (Singapore) **384-385** Designed by CREAM (Singapore) **386-387** Designed by Warren Liu and Darlene Smyth (Singapore); Photography by Rida Sobana/Courtesy of Warren Liu **388** Designed by James and Grace Tan (Singapore) **389-390** Designed by Draughtzman (Hong Kong) **391-392** Designed by Pichai-Theeranuj Wongwaisayawan (Bangkok) **393** Designed by Kelly Lee (Singapore)

index
índice
indice

CREAM (Singapore)
5 Purvis Street #01-01+02
Singapore 188584
t. (65) 6333 9115
f. (65) 6333 9116
e. creamhome@pacific.net.sg

CREAM Design + Architectural Planning
(Hong Kong)
12th Floor Capital Commercial Building
26 Leighton Road
Causeway Bay
Hong Kong
t. (852) 2147 1297
f. (331) 255 0152
e. info@cream.com.hk

Cu Fua Associates (Singapore)
325A Beach Road
Singapore 199559
t. (65) 6291 1172
f. (65) 6291 1792
e. cufua@pacific.net.sg

Cynosure Design Associates
(Singapore)
392A East Coast Road
Singapore 428992
t. (65) 6342 1200
f. (65) 6342 1500
e. george@cyno.com.sg

Dillon Garis Design Solutions (France)
5 rue du Pas de la Mule
75004 Paris
France
t. (331) 4272 5984
e. dillongaris@aol.com

Joey Ho (Hong Kong)
Room 202
2/F Union Commercial Building
12-16 Lyndhurst Terrace
Central, Hong Kong
t. (852) 2850 8732
f. (852) 2850 8972
e. joey@pointarchitects.com.hk

Hund & Pups (Singapore)
41 Defu Lane
Singapore 539430
t. (65) 6291 1258
f. (65) 6282 6879
e. jermaine@hundpups.com.sg

HYLA Architects (Singapore)
47 Ann Siang Road #02-01
Singapore 069720
t.(65) 6324 2488
f. (65) 6324 2466
e. admin@hyla.com.sg

Index Design Pte Ltd (Singapore)
15A Purvis Street
Singapore 188594
t. (65) 6220 1002
f. (65) 6334 7262
e.index@singnet.com.sg

MOIE (Singapore)
123 Penang Road
Regency House, Suite 01-13
Singapore 238465
t. (65) 6235 2260
f. (65) 6235 9391
e. moiesin@moie.com

OM Home (Singapore)
6 Raffles Boulevard
Marina Square #03-128
Singapore 039594
t. (65) 6457 0777
f. (65) 6883 1170
e. marina.square@om-home.com

POM/Peter Tay (Singapore)
7 Still Road South
Singapore 423924
t. (65) 6345 8142
f. (65) 6345 6036
e. pompom@asia.com

Room Interior Pte Ltd (Singapore)
15 Purvis Street
Singapore 188594
t. (65) 6333 9239
f. (65) 6333 9469
e. roominterior@pacific.net.sg

Weave Interior (Singapore)
44 Monk's Hill Road #03-48
Singapore 228575
t. (65) 6733 7585
f. (65) 6734 3171
e. weave@singnet.com

Whiz Concepts (Singapore)
25 Kreta Ayer Road
Singapore 088993
t. (65) 6372 1556
f. (65) 6372 1557
e. whizcon@cyberway.com.sg

Wide Open Spaces (Singapore)
57 Chartwell Drive
Singapore 558751
t. (65) 6289 8655
f. (65) 6289 6198
e. wos@swiftech.net.sg

Zong Architects (Singapore)
76 South Bridge Road
#04-00 Merchants Building
Singapore 058706
t. (65) 6226 0211
f. (65) 6223 1128
e. zongarch@singnet.com.sg

acknowledgments
agradecimientos
ringraziamenti

We would like to thank all the architects, designers for their kind permission to publish their works; all the photographers who have generously granted us permission to use their images; all our foreign co-ordinators – Anna Koor, Savinee Buranasilapin, Thomas Dannecker for their hard work and invaluable help; and most of all, to all the homeowners who have so graciously allow us to photograph their beautiful homes and to share them with readers the world over. Also, thank you to all those who have helped in one way or another in putting together this book. Thank you all.

La editorial da las gracias a todos los arquitectos y diseñadores que tan amablemente nos han dado permiso para publicar sus trabajos; a todos los fotógrafos que tan generosamente nos han permitido utilizar sus imágenes; a todos nuestros coordinadores en el extranjero (Anna Koor, Savinee Buranasilapin, Thomas Dannecker) por su intenso trabajo e inapreciable ayuda, y, en especial, a todos los propietarios de viviendas que tan gentilmente nos han permitido fotografiar sus preciosos hogares y compartirlos con lectores de todo el mundo. Asimismo damos las gracias a todos aquellos que han colaborado de una u otra forma en la realización de esta obra. Gracias a todos.

Desideriamo ringraziare tutti gli architetti e i designer che ci hanno gentilmente permesso di pubblicare le loro opere; tutti i fotografi che ci hanno generosamente concesso le loro foto; tutti i nostri coordinatori stranieri, Anna Koor, Savinee Buranasilapin, Thomas Danecker per il duro lavoro e l' enorme aiuto; e soprattutto tutti coloro che ci hanno cortesemente permesso di fotografare le loro meravigliose case, dividendole così con migliori di lettori in tutto il mondo. Grazie anche a tutti gli altri che in qualche modo ci hanno consentito di scrivere questo libro. Grazie a tutti.